The IEA Health and Welfare Unit

Choice in Welfare No. 15

The Family:
Is It Just Another Lifestyle Choice?

The IEA Health and Welfare Unit

Choice in Welfare No. 15

The Family: Is It Just Another Lifestyle Choice?

Jon Davies (Editor)

Brigitte Berger
Allan Carlson

IEA Health and Welfare Unit
London, 1993

First published in 1993
by
The IEA Health and Welfare Unit
2 Lord North St
London SW1P 3LB

ISBN 0-255 36276-5

Typeset by the IEA Health and Welfare Unit
in Palatino 11 on 12 point
Printed in Great Britain by
Goron Pro-Print Co. Ltd
Churchill Industrial Estate, Lancing, West Sussex

Contents

Foreword

The decline of the traditional family over the last generation or two has been unmistakeable. Lifelong loyalty of marriage partners is no longer the norm; each year tens of thousands of parents divorce before their children have grown up; and nearly one-third of births now take place outside marriage, with many of the fathers playing little or no further role after their initial biological participation. The traditional family of 'mum, dad and the kids' has become just another lifestyle choice.

Or so it seemed when this book was commissioned, but as the final preparations were under way it became obvious that a change in the national mood was taking place, triggered in part by the murder of a two-year old child in Liverpool allegedly at the hands of two ten-year olds from broken families. Many were asking, if child murder is the consequence of inadequate parenthood, is it not time to re-examine modern attitudes to family life?

For the last thirty years or so many intellectuals have been scornful of the traditional family, condemning it as the prime source of repression. This hostility derives from the view that freedom is about overcoming obstacles to our desires, from which it follows that we are free when we surmount any barriers standing in our way. To the middle-class intelligentsia, the most objectionable barrier of all is moral convention. They had spent their teenage years shouting, 'You can't tell me what to do' at their parents, and getting away with it, with the result that freedom for them meant defiance of authority, rebellion against established values.

Occasionally conventions deserve to be torn down and, in rapidly changing times, it is inevitable that each generation will cast a sceptical eye over the values it has inherited. What distinguishes the intelligentsia of the last 30 years is its inclination to condemn all conventions. The question that now confronts us is whether this antipathy to established values is endangering the free way of life which is the hallmark of Western civilisation.

Is every moral value just another lifestyle option? Or is there a minimum stock of values which we ignore at our peril? The chattering classes tend to dismiss concern about family breakdown by resorting to a well-tried list of stock phrases. The most popular is to accuse their opponents of 'moral panic'. Or, if anyone suggests that the traditional family should be restored, they are goaded with statements such as, 'You can't turn the clock back'; 'You can't put the genie back in the bottle'; or 'You can't put the toothpaste back in the tube'. Such claims amount to the absurd argument that we cannot learn from our mistakes. Moreover, the moral imperative that underpins the traditional family is really rather moderate. It is the view that children do not ask to be born, and that if a male and a female create a new human life, they should look after the child until he or she is grown up.

The same intellectuals who pour scorn on the family as repressive, also proclaim their support for a 'caring society'. But they have not understood that 'caring' begins in the family, and that if parents do not care sufficiently about their own children, why should they be expected to care about total strangers?

Renewed concern about the family is not confined to any one part of the spectrum of opinion. Powerful voices have been raised on the left. Most notable has been Professor A.H. Halsey, the distinguished Oxford sociologist. He is alarmed that so many children are born outside marriage and that the biological father often plays no part as a parent. In such cases, the father, Halsey has remarked with biting irony to a *Guardian* reporter, 'has never participated as a father but only as a genital'.

Halsey and his distinguished colleague Norman Dennis, co-author of the IEA paper, *Families Without Fatherhood*, focus their criticism on the failure of the now-dominant doctrine on the left, egoistic socialism. Its adherents are collectivists in economic policy but self-seeking in matters of personal lifestyle and morality, and look to the state to pick up the pieces left by their selfishness. For Halsey and Dennis this is an alarming departure from the tradition of ethical socialism to which they belong.

Halsey also targets the libertarianism of some free marketeers, who subscribe both to market economics and to 'anything goes' in personal lifestyle. There are free marketeers of this stripe, but they represent only one view among many. Another tradition, which might be called ethical capitalism, also takes the view that property rights and freedom of economic initiative are vital and indispensable pillars of a free society. But the ideal of ethical capitalists is not 'free markets' but 'liberty'. Their view was captured by Acton when he contrasted the 'realm of authority' with the 'realm of conscience'. To reduce the scope of the state, said Acton, was not to rely upon self-interest instead of state coercion, it was to rely on conscience instead of state power. Adam Smith, too, was quite clear about the driving force of a free society. In *The Theory of Moral Sentiments* he recognised that much could be accomplished by people pursuing their own interests and entering into mutually advantageous bargains, but the chief aim of individuals, he said, should not be their own gain, but Christian duty. Among these duties was the obligation to be a devoted father or mother and a respectful child.

Thus, public opinion on the family is now in a confused state. The die-hard nihilists have had their heyday and are now somewhat on the defensive, but they remain influential and continue to insist that nothing alarming is happening. All is well, they assert, and anyway, if there is more youth crime, then it is because of poverty and unemployment, not a decline in personal idealism or the quality of parenthood. This group includes intellectual feminists who write as if they regard the woman who goes out to work, however menial or intrinsically lacking in usefulness or satisfaction the job, as superior to the mother who devotes herself to raising her children as decent citizens. In their view, motherhood is nothing but drudgery; paid work is self-fulfilment. The die-hards are reinforced by the attitude of many well meaning but bewildered church leaders, including several bishops, who appear to be incapable of giving clear moral guidance.

The three papers in this collection of essays have been assembled in the hope of casting light on the widespread confusions surrounding discussion of the family. The IEA never expresses a corporate view, but in the light of Pascal's advice that the first moral obligation is to think clearly, these papers are highly commended as measured, scholarly contributions to one of the central, if still contentious, issues confronting the free societies of the West.

David G. Green

The Authors

Jon Davies is a Lecturer at the University of Newcastle upon Tyne, where he is Head of the Religious Studies Department. He was born in 1939 and educated in Kenya and later at Exeter College, Oxford, and Brandeis University, Mass., USA. He is married with three children. He was for nearly twenty years a Labour member of Newcastle City Council.

In 1972 he published *The Evangelistic Bureaucrat, a Study of a Planning Exercise in Newcastle upon Tyne* (Tavistock Press) and this year will be producing (co-edited with Isabel Wollaston of Birmingham University) *The Sociology of Sacred Texts*, Sheffield Academic Press. He has over the years written on *Municipal Capitalism*, Local Government Studies, 1987; *Asian Housing in Britain*, Social Affairs Unit, 1985; 'Duty and Self-sacrifice', in *The Loss of Virtue: Moral Confusion and Social Disorder in Britain and America*, Social Affairs Unit, (ed.) Digby Anderson, 1993. He lectures mainly on the liturgies, theologies and sociologies of marriage and death. He has in progress a book on war and war memorials.

Brigitte Berger, Professor of Sociology at Boston University, is the author of *Societies in Change, Childcare & Public Policy, The War Over the Family* and co-author of *Sociology: A Biographical Approach* and *The Homeless Mind*. Most recently she has been the editor of *The Culture of Entrepreneurship* and currently she is working on a book that relates micro social processes on the level of the family and community to large-scale issues of social change.

Allan Carlson is President of the Rockford Institute. He holds his PhD in Modern European History from Ohio University. Dr Carlson's books include: *From Cottage to Work Station: The Family's Search for Social Harmony in the Industrial Age*, 1993; *The Swedish Experiment in Family Politics: The Myrdals and the Interwar Population Crisis*, 1990; and *Family Questions: Reflections on the American Social Crisis*, 1988. In 1988 he was appointed by President Ronald Reagan as a member of the National Commission on Children, a position he held through 1992.

Introduction

The Family—R.I.P.?
Religion, Marriage, the Market and the State in Western Societies

Jon Davies

In *Family Socialisation and Interaction Process*, Talcott Parsons states that:

> the basic and irreducible functions of the family are two: the primary socialisation of the children so that they can truly become members of the society into which they have been born: second, the stabilisation of the adult personalities of the population of the society.[1]

It is clear from Parsons' writings (1) that he was talking about the monogamous nuclear family, (2) that he regarded such a family as the historical, statistical and moral norm in Western societies and (3) that even Parsons, the sociologist of 'structural differentiation; could see no possible further diminution of the functions of such a family unit: the two functions were 'irreducible'. Without them there neither would nor could *be* a Family. With and within The Family, and *only* with and within The Family, could children be socialised and young men and young women attain sexual and civic maturity.

These three papers address the increasingly obvious but still astonishing fact that since Parsons' time, large and increasing numbers of children no longer experience their primary socialisation in such a family unit and that adult personalities are decreasingly being 'stabilised' within the complementary gender role system of the stable nuclear family. The three authors, who are as will be seen, far from being agreed on everything, are agreed on at least one thing: that both the nature of these changes and their scale means that they are now matters of serious public rather than merely private concern. Changes in sexual and procreational behaviour are related to, and therefore affect, our economic, political and social life. While the three papers reveal considerable differences in judgement as to what exactly is happening, and why, and what if anything could or should be done about it, all three authors agree that on the basis of the evidence we have, there is no better alternative to a stable nuclear family as a way both of socialising children and of effecting the transition to maturity of young men and young women.

The three papers were discussed at a Liberty Fund Symposium held in Cambridge in September 1992. This Symposium covered a wide variety of views indeed, and no single participant is in any way responsible for the views expressed in this volume, which are those of the Editor and authors only. Amongst the Symposium participants, however, were an author and an editor of two recent Institute of Economic Affairs' books on the family, both published in 1992: Norman Dennis, co-author with George Erdos of *Families Without Fatherhood* and Caroline Quest, editor of and contributor to *Equal Opportunities: A Feminist Fallacy*. These books, and this volume, are published in the context of a culture which is quite profoundly sceptical about and hostile to the very notion of the stable nuclear family. Our culture seems to be casually experimenting with a wide range of procreational, familial, and nurturing practices. There are families without fathers, to use the title of Norman Dennis' and George Erdos' recent book,[2] mothers without husbands, men without children, marriages without permanence, love without fidelity, self-interest without self-denial. Allan Carlson's question (see below) 'Does Liberty Rest on Strong Families?' would in the present climate no doubt elicit the response: 'No! Liberty consists of being free of and from strong families, for they (strong families) are the historic location of oppression and exploitation, and if such families are indeed being undermined or abolished, then so much the better!' In particular, it is argued by many feminists, the family which Parsons presented as the norm is an ideological construct, in reality nothing more than the location of patriarchy, a place where men, and men only, obtain and have power, and where all patterns of socialisation and maturity are a distorting and bending of infant, juvenile and female natures into the phallocentric world of men. 'Research into gender' writes Angela Phillips, 'shows that it is fathers, not mothers, who reinforce gender roles in the family'— and this statement is advanced (on the Parents Page of *The Guardian*) as proving that socialisation into male gender roles by males present in The Family is incontestably and self-evidently a Bad Thing. For this reason, continued Angela Phillips, the sundering of the father-male role at times of divorce was in no way to be seen as an argument against divorce:—'clearly the most important component of the parental relationship is not gender...boys can learn to be men from other sources'.[3]

Most divorce in Great Britain is initiated by women, indicating (so it is said) that men are at best inadequate and recalcitrant conscripts to domestication and at worst, and perhaps by nature, barbarians, incapable of authentic non-exploitative relationships, and therefore now quite deservedly left on the shelf in what is for the first time in our history a genuine market in sexual and procreational affairs.

The three papers in this volume seek to understand not only what is happening—i.e. to establish The Facts about matters such as the rate of teenage pregnancy or of birth outside marriage or the consequences (for society, for either parent or for children) of divorce and single-parenthood—but also why it is that such changes seem to be so sought after by so many people, in particular (if the divorce-initiation patterns are anything to go by) by so many women, of whom many are mothers, for whom (and for whose children) both divorce and motherhood without a partner are frequently associated with considerable anguish and a lower than average standard of living. Are these women deluded and irresponsible, seduced by the power of feminist messages in the media? Or are men so detestable as partners that many women, now that for the first time in our history we have something rather like a genuine marriage market, are opting out of it? And what are the social consequences of the changes that are being so zealously welcomed? What are the causes of these changes? Is state intervention to be blamed for whatever is going wrong—or to be praised for whatever is going right? Is 'the market', when defined as the pursuit of individual self-interest, now so deeply ingrained in our culture that it permeates even intra-familial relationships, hitherto seen as precisely the location of altruistic or other-regarding rather than self-regarding relationships—or is that formulation yet another piece of masculine ideology and self-delusion, an invocation of a Golden Age which never really existed?

Sexual and procreational relationships in the past had been heavily rooted in religious teaching: marriage and family life had been sacralised. Can it be re-sacralised? If The Family as an institution derived its moral force from religious precepts and church surveillance, can it be re-sacralised now that the precepts are unknown or ignored, when the church is unattended and when God is dead? What can be done, by anyone who would seek to try, to re-establish a moral doctrine through which men and women define their very sense of maturity in their behaviour as wife and husband, mother and father, when we live in a world in which 'style, fashion and taste have replaced guilt, morality and notions of right and wrong'?[4]

The stable nuclear family, as my own paper makes clear, was rooted in a coherent sexual ethic which restricted sexual activity to marital procreational sex alone. How practical an option is this in a world which sells sex via Madonna?

The labour market is changing. If the male role derived (in part) from an employment system requiring male muscle, and from a labour market assuming that married women were at home, then what happens to those roles now that the muscle-requiring jobs have gone, when 60 per cent of married women work, and when all predictions of labour requirements in the future point to more jobs for women than for men? Will wages in such a labour market develop spontaneously to cope with changing 'family' needs? If, as the authors agree, women have certain natural advantages as mother-parents, is full-time work for women thereby ruled out, and is part-time work acceptable? Whether men or women are at work, and whether recourse is had to the market or to the state, does the availability of pensions via insurance schemes, whereby one generation can actually provide for its own old age, constitute a major break in those patterns of mutual need which so underwrote (and perhaps strained) relationships between the generations in the past? What, now, are the material bases of inter-generational transactions when children are so expensive to have and to maintain and where there is little in actuality or in our moral culture which will predictably oblige them to return the financial favour when they are themselves 'the earners'? We are surely unique in that the wealth possessed (by inheritance or creation) by one generation could, if used only for itself, provide for its own 'old age'. The pension plans of one generation are a contract with itself, and if this is the only contract it needs, why—except for sentimental reasons—should the next generation honour its mothers and fathers?

In our society sex is held to be pre-eminently the private domain, and in as much as family life is sexual life, then it too lays claim to all the privileges of privacy, an area held to be necessarily and properly free of all societal as well as state control, interference or even comment. 'A woman's right to choose' lays down with absolute clarity the freedom of the physical from the control of the Word—be they church words, or legal words, or social words. A woman's right to choose, it is held, extends not only to herself but also to her children so that the divorce or single parenthood increasingly sought by women is presented as either beneficial for them as well as for her, or if beneficial only for her, then at least neutral in its effects on her children.

Indeed, so strong is the belief in the autonomy of the consenting adult that his or her freedom of action is held to be legitimate even when there are clear public costs and consequences—see Norman Dennis' notion of egoistic socialism in the book referred to above. In the debates about the family there is a general although not total agreement that family disruption and an increase in poverty are correlated. The disagreement is about the direction of the causality and, associated with that, an argument about the appropriate public response. If, say, single-parent households are poor, should they be advised to marry or remarry (and everyone else advised or compelled not to get into the never-married or divorced condition in the first place) or should we (SOCIETY) be invited or compelled to provide them and their children with more money, on the assumption that it is 'only' the lack of money that is the problem and that there is no economic, social or moral reason why such costs should not be carried collectively? It is clear that in the past sexual behaviour, most obviously and most easily the sexual behaviour of women, was to a very great extent controlled by a system of stigma and punishment, or reward and accolade. As with the idea of re-sacralising domesticity—how re-institutable is such a system?

The most influential view these days is that the variety of sexual and procreational 'relationships' with which we are experimenting are merely variants of family life (and even benign variants) and that the costs of providing for them are legitimate calls on the public purse. Further, it is held that the rather evident social problems of our society (such as high crime rates or problematic behaviour at school) are the result not of such experiments *per se* but of poverty and/or inadequate levels of welfare expenditure. Less attention is paid to the argument that we may be seeing in much contemporary behaviour a clue to what may happen on a broad scale when men are both unemployed and detached from stable family life, as compared to earlier periods when unemployment rates were higher and poverty deeper, but when both crime rates and rates of family breakdown were dramatically lower. If the variable that made, and makes, the difference is the incidence of stable nuclear families, then should divorce be made harder (perhaps by re-introducing the idea of the marital offence), marriage more popular (even sacred) or more difficult (perhaps by requiring the taking out of a divorce insurance policy), and illegitimacy and sexual permissiveness more stigmatised? Generally, and essentially, is it not the case that procreational decisions are not and cannot be matters of purely private concern, and that no matter what problem human beings find themselves in over their life-time, no problem (sexual or otherwise) is made easier by separating men from women, wives from husbands, children from parents. Whatever hole you are in, digging it deeper does not help, surely?

But the occupants of the hole are not the only ones who are digging. Alan Carlson (see below) argues that various state interventions, in particular the imposition of compulsory state education, have been among the major causes of the weakening of the independent nuclear family. I, on the other hand, take the view that this century has seen the dismantling of a centuries-old system of state regulation of procreational matters, and that the seductive forces of the market and the media are what are causing the instability in inter-sex and inter-generational relationships. Brigitte Berger, more optimistic than either Carlson or me, takes the middle line that problems derive from both state intervention and market forces, from the cushions of collective provision as well as from the blandishments of individualism—but that the good sense of ordinary people could be relied upon to correct the present excesses and restore support for what are to her (and to the other two authors) the evident practical advantages of the traditional stable nuclear family. It is clear to all three authors that our free and reasonably successful society will be able to remain free and stable only when each generation moves into its maturity and its civic responsibilities when it has effectively internalised those values which make for freedom and stability. The only institution which can provide the time, the attention, the love and the care for doing that is not just 'the family', but a stable two-parent mutually complementary nuclear family. The fewer of such families that we have, the less we will have of either freedom or stability.

Notes

1 Parsons, T., 1956, p. 16.

2 Dennis, N. and Erdos, G., *Families Without Fatherhood*, IEA Health and Welfare Unit, London: 1992.

3 *The Guardian*, 23 October 1992.

4 French, Phillip, reviewing Woody Allen's film 'Husbands and Wives', the *Observer*, 25 October 1992.

The Bourgeois Family and Modern Society

Brigitte Berger

There can be little doubt that between roughly 1400 and 1800 the modern world—with its enormous dynamic potential and its destructive capacity—emerged in Europe and, more specifically, in North-Western Europe. Why *there* and why *then* are two questions that have preoccupied social thinkers since the days of Adam Smith and today most analysts tend to agree with Alexis de Tocqueville that the rise of the modern world is a consequence of peculiar institutional arrangements which find their clearest expression in the capitalist economy, political democracy and individual liberty. In present-day analyses of the economy, the law, education, the class structure and the like it is taken for granted that these institutions constitutive of modern society are 'functionally' interrelated and dependent upon each other. What, precisely these linkages are and the ways in which they are anchored in society remains elusive and the subject of debate.

This paper seeks to contribute to this debate by identifying some key factors that have been instrumental in the rise of democracy, capitalism, and individual liberty. On the basis of evidence from historical and contemporary comparative research it will be argued that all the institutions of modern society have common sources and, more specifically, that these common sources must be located in the individualistic familism of the 'bourgeois' family, its ethos, and the moral communities engendered by it.

To say this is not to deny the value of other family forms. There is little doubt that the family in a great variety of forms stands at the core of every society, be it the family of antiquity, of exotic groups in remote corners of the globe, or in the teeming centres of contemporary Third World urban conglomerations. However, recent research findings strongly suggest that it has been the nuclear family of father, mother and children, living and working together, tied to each other by mutual affection and a very distinctive ethos—to which the somewhat ambiguous label the 'bourgeois family' has been attached—which has engendered processes making for the development of modern institutions, including those of the polity and the economy. In this sense, this type of family has contributed more to history than is commonly understood for it is the culture-creating institution of modernity *par excellence*. In fact, a good argument can be made that the bourgeois family has been the *only* institution sufficiently dynamic to engender the social processes making for both modernization and economic development.

At the same time, it has to be remembered that culture is a living and vividly human process. If it can be shown that the institutions of modern society have their origin in particular family processes and structures—as I think it can—it follows that for industrial liberal democracies to flourish, it is exceedingly import-ant to recognize that similar familial processes, along with the moral structures of the communities in which they are embedded, continue to play an important, if not indispensable role in their future as well. And this proposition takes us to what in a different context I have called 'the war over the family'. For today, it is precisely the 'bourgeois' family which has become a problem. Far-reaching shifts in the organization of human sexuality, in the relationship between husbands and wives, parents and children, in the persistent encroachment of the state and its agents into ever more niches of private life along with the ever-present lure of a consumer culture created by the capitalist market have made the bourgeois family vulnerable to an extraordinary degree.

Now this may be an unfamiliar way of looking at things. Wherever one turns today one encounters the argument for the primacy of structure and structural constellations—the technology, the economy, the law and so forth—from which everything else flows. In this view, the family, in its form as well as its content, is determined by factors of the social structure, or, in the jargon of the social sciences, the family is a 'dependent' rather than an 'inde-pendent' variable. That is to say, individual and familial well-being is held to be dependent upon structural arrangements. If structural shifts appear to place undue pressures upon families, or more precisely, upon particular types of families—as for instance those flowing from increases in divorce, teenage parenthood, female participation in the labour force and so forth—then it falls upon the government and its agencies to counteract the 'fall-out' of such shifts. Beyond that, it has become standard practice among social scientists and policy advocates to insist on the 'inclusive' use of the term 'family'. In official communications and documents reference is invariably made to the breadth of all sorts of 'family' configurations, including biological kin networks and non-related persons who consider themselves to be family through a 'network of mutual commitment', all equally valid if not desirable.

The defenders of the 'bourgeois family', typically referred to as the 'traditional family', are not only thought to have fallen prey to a myth to begin with (as it is alleged never to have existed in its pure form), but, given contemporary structural shifts, it is argued, that this type of family can neither serve as a social norm nor is it worthy of support. Whatever support can be made available has to be reserved for the 'victims' of structural 'fall out'. That is to say, not only is the culture-creating force of the bourgeois family denied flat out, but what is rejected as well is the proposition that individual hopes and social values are able to transcend the parameters of social structure. By extension, there exists today a widespread conviction that it is the social structure that determines what is to be normative. That what is, is what ought to be. This position, I would claim, is not only empirically and philosophically questionable, but what is more, it puts the future of our kind of society into considerable peril.

Before presenting arguments in support of my core proposition, a few words about the use of the term 'bourgeois family' are in order. In a different context I have argued against the imprisonment of the bourgeois phenomenon in Marxist terminology and, in particular, against the pejorative consequences of such ideological labels. Few self-respecting scholars today will use terms like 'bourgeois democracy' and 'bourgeois family' without distancing themselves from the reality both purport to denote. Few, if any, are prepared as well to attribute much public value to the 'bourgeois virtues' of frugality, enterprise, decency, common sense, abstinence, discipline, reliability, politeness, respect for others and a general sense of fairness, all typically associated with the behaviour of the individual. Consonant with the espoused structural approach, they prefer to locate 'the root causes' (a give-away phrase if there ever was one) of individual and social problems in the structure, rather than in individual patterns of behaviour. Needless to say, this tendency has put the social fabric of Western societies under considerable pressure in recent decades.

Simon Schama in his *The Embarrassment of Riches*[1], a brilliant interpretation of Dutch culture in the Golden Age, vociferously argues against the clichéd use of the term 'bourgeois' which he finds to profoundly misrepresent its culture and values. He suggests that if 'bourgeois' is translated into *burgerlijk* as the Dutch do,—or 'buergerlich' as the Germans do, one may add—more is altered than just the linguistic form. The economic emphasis, invariably associated with the term in Marxist interpretations of capitalism, would then promptly shift to include its 'civic' dimension. A novel combination of new economically productive behaviour patterns, a growing civic consciousness and an intensified respect for individuals and their rights, is precisely what sets the bourgeois family apart from the 'amoral familism' (the term is Edward Banfield's) characteristic of traditional societies regardless of time and space. It is this combination of factors that led to the birth of 'a new manner of life' and lent a revolutionary thrust to the bourgeois family.

To appreciate the felicity of Schama's suggestion, it is important to keep in mind that modernization is a process distinct from economic development. It not only refers to changes in the social, economic, and political structures of society but, above all, to changes in the structure of the consciousness of individuals: their ideas, values, and hopes. While it can plausibly be argued that the onset of industrial production dramatically transformed all aspects of social life, including consciousness, it is hard to maintain that this particular form of production appeared suddenly out of nowhere. History has shown that modernization is the result of long historical processes in the West which included far-reaching changes in human consciousness. Indeed, if industrialization caused great changes in consciousness, the advent of industrialization was itself rooted in specific changes in consciousness (such as individuation and rationalization, both of which, if Max Weber was right, may go back as far as the origins of the Judeo-Christian worldview).

If one accepts this line of argument, then one is propelled to push the question further yet and inquire into the processes that made for a significant shift in the consciousness of large numbers of ordinary individuals, and not just a select few. What is at issue here is the identification of a peculiar *modern* form of consciousness and how it became anchored in society at large. To pose the question in this way takes us back to the theme of this paper, namely the recovery of the civilatory mission of the bourgeois, or middle-class, family if you will. For there can be little doubt that there exists a continuum between private virtues and public actions and I would propose, the bourgeois home provides the basis and anchor to both.

At the danger of subjecting the reader to what may perhaps be an overly detailed discussion of the foundations of all institutions, including those of modernity, let me make only a brief excursus into sociological theory in the Weberian mode. At the methodological core of Max Weber's sociology is the attempt to understand (*verstehen*) the meaning of human actions. Man, in this view, is the meaning-giving animal *par excellence*. No observer can understand man's behaviour unless he understands the meaning that gives rise to the behaviour. This, in the fullest sense of the word, is a humanizing perspective. It makes one cautious in speaking of systems, structures, functions, mechanisms, even institutions. All these are human artifacts, human constructions, which have no ontological status apart from the meaningful actions that created them. Robert McIver, one of the most Weberian of American sociologists, once used a very graphic analogy to make this point. He referred to the Biblical story according to which the Israelites were victorious in a battle only as long as Aaron and Hur held up Moses' hands. The institutions of a human society only exist as long as living human beings hold them up by their actions. In that sense, finally, there are no institutions; there is no one here but us people.

Thus, if one is to understand the political, economic and cultural institutions of modern society, it is not enough to think of systems, structures and the like. One must look 'behind', or 'beneath', these artifacts in order to perceive the living human beings who make these artifacts work. To put it differently, this is a perspective 'from the bottom up'—the 'bottom' being the everyday reality of living human beings. That reality, as I have argued, is defined by the ways in which individuals in families embedded in their communal structures try to give purpose to their actions and make sense out of human life.

Theoretical discussions such as these notwithstanding, anyone who has eyes to see must admit that recent history has not been kind to the bourgeois family. Disregarded and ultimately by-passed by those who came to dominate in the political arena, increasingly maligned by the carriers of the 1960's counter culture, it has frequently been turned into an object of ridicule. At the same time, however, massive research demonstrates beyond the shadow of a doubt that by far the majority of ordinary people continue to be guided in their daily lives and their hopes for the future by bourgeois norms. To be sure, in this instance as in many others, reality frequently falls short of the ideal. Yet the ideal itself prevails largely intact. The same body of research has made it evident as well, that a family consisting of a father and a mother, living together and being actively involved with the well-being and achievements of their children is still the single best guarantee for an individual's success in school and in life beyond. As the findings are too well documented to be ignored completely, the past decade has witnessed a new, though grudging, public recognition of the significance of the 'traditional' family.

On closer scrutiny, however, this recognition, remains more along the line of paying lip-service —similar to a routine genuflection before a long-forgotten idol—rather than giving substance to it. Regardless of whatever political philosophy may inform the social policies of Western governments, it appears that deeply ensconced anti-family sentiments continue to carry the day, much to the dismay of the defenders of the bourgeois family like myself. No good would be served by recapitulating these arguments here. Permit me, however, to return to my core proposition and try to substantiate and expand it with the help of 'case' materials from historical and recent cross-cultural research.

The Examples of Bourgeois Familism

Case 1: The 'Bourgeois Family' as the Source of Modernity

Let me begin with the most central proposition of the argument, namely that a family-anchored 'new manner of life' is the basis of modernity, that the elements constitutive of the 'bourgeois' family are the precondition rather than the consequence of modernization and economic development.

How can this possibly be, you may ask. From childhood on, we have been taught precisely the opposite. Schools and newspapers and broadcasters lead us to think of the nuclear form of the family as the consequence of the destructive forces of industrialization and urbanization. Social historians such as Karl Polanyi have confirmed a whole generation of academic writers in that assumption. What is more, for far too many people, this type of family, with its insistence upon individual responsibility, achievement orientation, and civic commitments is more of an aberration to be overcome rather than an ideal to be emulated.

This assumption, however, is no longer tenable today. A large body of detailed historical materials collected in recent decades by social demographers and historians around Peter Laslett and Alan Macfarlane in England, on the European continent in France, Germany, Switzerland and Austria, and in North America, strongly suggests that the Western nuclear family flourished long before the advent of industrialization. Alan Macfarlane in particular has explored the continuity between social practices over the centuries.[2] In locating the origins of English individualism long before the onset of industrial production, tying this individualism to firm notions of private property, and political independence, he was able to adumbrate attitudes in large parts of the population that came to be the carriers of particular forms of consciousness we typically associate with modernity. To be sure, the complicated processes whereby sentiments and practices on the micro-level of society, i.e. the family, provided the basis for distinctly modern institutions, has not yet been sufficiently explored. We still have to await more systematic treatments of how individual habits and practices become institutionalized and thereby provide the structural patterns. However this may be, I think we can confidently assume that the inner dynamics of family and community life played a pivotal role in the rise of a new social order.

Few case studies are better suited to reveal the 'inner dynamics' of the Western nuclear family than Rudolf Braun's research on 'The Demographic Transition of the Canton Zurich in the 18th and 19th Century'. The transition itself was fuelled by the inner dynamics of the 'proto-industrial household', a type of household that best applies to that segment of rural artisans and peasants engaged in the cottage work system of 'putting out' typically connected to the emergent textile industry of that period. Braun's historical description provides us with an unique opportunity to glean the interactive relationship between family-rooted patterns of behaviour, values, beliefs, and thought on the one hand, and a new type of productive activity that became available at that time.

On the *individual level*, the putting-out system provided for the first time opportunities for individualized courtship, marriage, and the creation of one's own domestic sphere. Moreover, the establishment of a home of one's own, the creation of one's own little world—referred to as the proto-industrial household in social science literature—was the desired way of life for many. Since it was available to anyone who cared to take it up, it was potentially democratic. It emphasized hard work, frugality, honesty, saving, rational planning and the instrumental role of individuals and their unique contributions. The new patterns of behaviour and work emerging in this fashion from a household-centred form of production rendered tangible results relatively quickly and came to serve as a model to be emulated by many. It may be of some importance to note that the newly emerging way of life did not appeal to those embedded in the traditional structures of peasant life and land ownership, rather, the proto-industrial household became the 'preferred option' of the poor, the underprivileged classes, the marginal and roving segment of the population at that time.

On the *structural level* this type of household production fostered new structures of consciousness and practices, which, when put into action on a large scale, were precisely those that served as necessary preambles to the industrial revolution. At the same time, the proto-industrial household was compelled to move beyond the confines of the immediate family and kinship circle. In order to flourish it had to establish new networks of interaction and trust, which in subsequent periods allowed for the emergence of separate spheres of action and responsibility.

It is also important to note that both family dynamics and work dynamics were activated and reinforced by a very distinctive personal ethic—the much celebrated 'Protestant Ethic' made famous by Max Weber as modernization's 'enabling' force. Under the influence of this ethos the bourgeois family gave birth to modern structures of consciousness which provided a felicitous balance between an 'amoral familism' and an increasingly dynamic civic responsibility, between individual autonomy and individual achievement on the one had, and an ever-expanding cooperation on the other. Slowly and incrementally, the elements constitutive of this new manner of life became habituated, routinized, and eventually institutionalized. The new ethos of modernity enabled individuals and their groups to transcend the limitations of frequently stifling traditions and other obstacles in an often hostile world. In this fashion ordinary individuals, in their habits, practices, and ideas, created the basis for other distinctly modern institutions to emerge that mediate between them and the distant, large-scale structures of society. It is *this* culture that created the modern world.

It would, of course, be foolish to deny the importance of external conditions of production and technology as well as the many legal and political factors which contributed to the rise of the modern world. Yet the type of historical transformation revealed in Rudolf Braun's and similar research efforts brings into view an interconnectedness between events on the micro-level of society and the large macro-structures on the one hand, and the singular importance of factors of culture, on the other. And here it becomes necessary to add a caveat on the significance of cultural propensities which will protect us from falling into some sort of self-congratulatory ethnocentricism.

On the one hand, it may be argued that socio-cultural development embodies a rational and universal human ability, theoretically available in any human group at any time. On the other hand, an examination of the world map of economic development and modernization illuminates what has become a truism by now: namely, some cultures appear to be more conducive to modernization and development. The culture-propensity argument has been used for a long time to explain the rise of some European societies to economic and political pre-eminence. While out of fashion during 1960s and 1970s, the culture-propensity argument has been revived recently, particularly in connection with attempts that seek to explain the spectacular rise of the societies of the Pacific Rim. After having explored exhaustively the relative significance of all sorts of variables, most analysts today arrive at the rock-bottom insight that Japanese, Korean, and Chinese culture—in spite of vast differences—are particularly well-suited for the present 'stage' of industrialization.

To be sure, recent developments in East Asia call for a revision of Max Weber's path-breaking attempts at cultural analysis that sought to explain differential rates of modernization in Europe in terms of differences between the Calvinist and the Catholic ethic. And in the preceding historical case of the family connection in the proto-industrial economy of the early 19th century Swiss Canton, I would also call for an expansion and modification of the Weberian core proposition. But contemporary research around the globe once more moves the importance of explanations of culture *a la* Weber into the centre of the debate.

While culture must be taken seriously, it is also of utmost importance to handle the concept of culture with great care. Above all, it has to be shorn of the romantic myth that entire civilizations are predestined to advance and others are condemned to lag behind. If, however, one *disaggregates the notion of cultural totality* into straightforward, rational, and empirically researchable variables, it becomes possible to identify some of the constitutive features and constellations that are at work in any culture at any time. On the basis of this procedure it then becomes possible to assess which factors and constellations are likely to make for change, modernization, and economic development while, at the same time, identifying those that lead to stagnation or 'involution' to use Clifford Geertz's term. In the course of such a procedure, I would propose, the civilatory mission of highly particularistic family processes and patterns analogous to those found to be typical of the bourgeois pattern, regardless of place and historical time, move into focus.

Case 2: The Family-Based Dynamics of Third World Urban Migration

Modern day observers have frequently asked to what degree the history of the European transformation may serve as a useful analogy for contemporary Third World societies. In what follows I wish to propose that the family-fuelled dynamic just described is not confined to the West alone. Today we can observe similar transformations taking place in cultures as far apart as Brazil and Chile in Latin America and Hong Kong at the opposite side of the globe. However, the scope and implications of these processes are insufficiently understood as of yet. The shifts currently occurring in many parts of the world involve the movement of often desperately poor people from rural areas into the *barrios* and *favellas* of Latin America, the shanty towns of Africa, and the steaming cities of Asia.

Here in hostile environments, frequently living in abject poverty, these migrants have prevailed against all the odds. Unwanted and unaided, lacking in resources and skills, these poorest of the world's poor have been thrown back upon their own resilience and ingenuity. In their efforts to survive they were typically driven into the economic underground, the 'informal sector', where by means of self-help entrepreneurial activities on the smallest level they have engendered socio-economic patterns of interaction and established rudimentary social structures, almost accidentally as it were, that hold considerable potential for the future of their countries.

At the centre of these major transformations stand family, household and entrepreneurship, strongly reminiscent of the Western case just discussed. Knowledgeable analysts of contemporary Chilean, Peruvian and Brazilian events, for instance, argue that a dynamic potential exists at the bottom of these societies, waiting to be unleashed. Hernando de Soto, in his *The Other Path*,[3] (based on detailed studies among Lima's urban migrants and squatters) makes a strong case for the recognition of the economic potential of this vast segment of the population. Similar data from across the world suggest that, under specific conditions and aided by a proto-modern ethos, the as yet uncharted economic and social activities of the urban migrants to Third World cities may provide the 'engine' for their society's transformation.

A growing number of studies have focused on a variety of dimensions of Third World urban poverty. So for instance, some have looked at the importance of social relationships in the search for shelter, the construction of housing, the migrants' search for work, loans, and insurance. Others have looked for changes in family relationships, and others, again, have explored the emergence of neighbourhood and voluntary organization, particularly those of a religious nature. In almost all cases I had occasion to survey in some depth, it became evident that the urban migrants were able to engender forms of social relationships that were distinctly different from those they had been born into and raised.

The process of migration and adaption to novel urban contexts expose the new urbanites to experiences of dislocation and uprootedness. At the same time, these very same experiences also posed a fundamental challenge to the viability of behaviour patterns and modes of thought embedded in traditional structures of family and community. While the value and the reality of a family, a household, and a community remain paramount, tradition as such no longer is able to inform individual practices adequately and leaves them open to find more appropriate ways. By definition almost, individuals cannot achieve such a reorientation by themselves. Whatever reorientation takes place, occurs within the context of the family which now gains a significance it did not have before. Not only does the family remain the one and only 'haven in a heartless world', it also provides the locale and the instruments for redefining the life of an individual and his family itself. In a paradoxical manner, the family now reconstitutes itself.

Thus liberated from tradition the family comes, as it were, into its own and gains new and added significance for individuals and society alike. In studies by sociologists like Bernard Rosen, whose *The Industrial Connection*[4] presents us with a welcome point of entry into the discussion, we see today a family in formation in the *favellas* of Brazilian cities whose interdependent mode of production and normative requirements makes for a strengthening rather than a weakening of kinship ties, increases husband-wife relationships and communication, and brings into focus the importance of achievement oriented socialization and education.

And again analogous to the European case, a 'new manner of life' appears to be in the making at the intersection of family, work and a particular—revolutionary if you will—ethos. When all is said and done and one has controlled for the exotic quality of the setting, what is revealed here once more is the instrumental role of behaviour and value patterns originating in what we may call a proto-bourgeois family dynamic which trendy publicists tend to malign. And reminiscent of the Western case as well, we observe the singular importance of a new religiously informed ethic in this fundamental shift.

In his pathbreaking book *Tongues of Fire* the British sociologist David Martin[5] documents the importance of Pentecostal and fundamentalist sects in the revolutionary transformation currently occurring in Brazil. Like similar studies before him, Martin's research findings strengthen once more the important insight of a generation of earlier scholars that modern society, in order to prosper, must not only be a moral community—other societies are that too—but a moral community of a particular kind. The harsh fundamentalist ethos requires of its disciples self-control, discipline, hard work, sobriety, self-reliance, frugality, saving, along with all the other 'bourgeois virtues' alluded to earlier. In what may be called a 'domestication of the senses', sexual appetites are tamed, inclinations toward self indulgence are disciplined, self-gratification is postponed and a new general appreciation of how present behaviour may influence an individual's future prospects makes its entry. Basic to all of these sentiments and new activities is the unwavering desire of women and men to create a stable basis for the survival and the advancement of their families.

These new family relationships go hand in hand with entrepreneurial activities, albeit on the smallest scale. Virtually all studies on the life of the Third World urban poor show that self-help activities prevail in almost every sphere of social life. Indeed, the urban poor would be unable to survive without such attempts at helping themselves. Small-scale entrepreneurs, however, seem to have a particularly strong propensity for self-help activities of a great variety. Not only do they develop considerable ingenuity and skills in the uncovering of new economic activities, they also appear to develop similar skills in the uncovering and establishment of a market for their products and services. That fact alone makes even more persuasive those arguments that claim that very few of the small enterprises could survive without developing stable relationships of dependence with customers, suppliers, neighbours and larger enterprises in order to obtain credit or to secure stable markets for their products. Although the independence of small-scale entrepreneurs is fragile, their own participation in forming and sustaining all sorts of networks of relationships enables them to retain a degree of control of their own situation.

Much of the literature emphasises the importance of ethnic networks. Thus, it has been observed that people from the same village tend to live together in the same neighbourhood in the city and to help each other in business if they are able. This applies equally to the cooked food vendors of Latin American cities, the doll makers of the Philippines as to the ethnic operators of subway news-stands and vegetable stores in New York City. Ethnic groups establish mutual support structures, which can include rudimentary insurance systems in case of illness, revolving loan funds and assistance in obtaining licenses. At times spontaneously formed neighbourhood groups actively protest against local authorities and governments.

Many of the small-scale entrepreneurs engaged in the 'penny capitalism' of the household economy are women. The women often supply the entrepreneurial skills, the hard labour, the stamina, and the unwavering desire for creating a stable basis for the survival and the advancement of their families. Policy makers and economists have paid scant attention to the contributions of the familial focus that guides the Third World migrant. What they have failed to recognize in particular is that their economic activities are less driven by 'rational actor' factors as by values relating to family and family life, which frequently may not be so rational in economic terms. It is one of the merits of the new research on women in development to have tried to fill this lacuna. Yet feminists too have failed to apprehend the family connection in all of this. Like economists, their focus has been on the isolated autonomous woman and her contribution and place in the economy. But an autonomous woman, who coolly and rationally is concerned only with her own self-interests, is a phenomenon unknown in the Third World.

Case 3: Hong Kong's Entrepreneurial Familism

Anyone who has been to Hong Kong in recent years cannot fail but be overwhelmed by the dynamism of this tiny urban colony at the tip of the Chinese mainland. Study after study, particularly those by S.L. Lau, Gilbert Wong and S. Gordon Redding, celebrate the centrality of a Chinese 'entrepreneurial familism' in Hong Kong's spectacular success, a familism typical of countless Chinese migrants to the Colony that provides the foundation, the engine, and the goal of the wealth-producing activities.

To refer here to Hong Kong's dynamic familism, however, is not to illustrate once more the economic contribution of family collaboration—the above cases, I think, have already sufficiently done so. What needs to be brought out more clearly at this point, is how the political organization of the economy can squash the dynamic potential only families possess. Furthermore, what needs to be pointed out as well is that any ethos that in its constitutive components is analogous to that of the Protestant ethic, is able to constructively channel the institution-building potential of the family. That is to say, Westerners have to take great care not to become fixated on the singular role of the Protestant ethic. Whatever this ethos may be, however, it must be rooted in and revolve around the family. In his fascinating *The Spirit of Chinese Capitalism*, S. Gordon Redding documents in great detail the interaction between Chinese familism and the Confucian ethic that has turned Hong Kong into one of the preeminent economic centres of the world.[6] One of Redding's most poignant conclusions 'no capitalist development without an entrepreneurial class; no entrepreneurial class without a moral charter; no moral charter without religious premises' is worth repeating here. It reveals not only the cultural foundations of the modern economic order, but also points to the prerequisites needed for the creation of a modern entrepreneurial class. And this takes us to the dynamics peculiar to the Chinese family.

According to conventional social science thinking, familism and economic development are antipathetic. With regard to Chinese familism itself, the opinions of contemporary social scientists have by and large echoed Max Weber's famous phrase of the 'sib fetters of the economy'. Thus negative evaluations have not only been accepted by many Western scholars for a long time, but they also have influenced Chinese elites throughout the twentieth century. Communist as well as non-communist Chinese elites were convinced that the core values of the Chinese family—revolving around family solidarity, patrilineal descent and ancestor worship, patriarchal authority and filial piety requiring obedience to the father and allegiance and loyalty to the emperor—were profoundly anti-modern and presented a major stumbling block to China's progress. The communist regime, under Mao in particular, undertook draconian measures to smash the kinship-oriented structure of traditional Chinese society, with devastating consequences, as we now know.

The new research, however, reveals the precise opposite. Max Weber, we know today, was wrong. Once liberated from the interference of political authorities and unleashed in Hong Kong's *laissez-faire* economic milieu, the very same structures, values, and dynamics provided the basis for the Colony's success. On the basis of detailed research among migrants from the mainland into Hong Kong, Gilbert Wong of Hong Kong University, has demonstrated carefully and with great precision how this became possible. He shows compellingly how the Chinese family has been an economically active force not only today but, what is more, he argues that it had that potential in the past as well. In former times, however, this potential was checked by a state preoccupied with efforts to balance perceived economic, environmental and ecological factors, which to many contemporary analysts were seriously misguided as they locked a whole society into a 'high level equilibrium trap.' Once such external pressures were removed, the inner dynamics of the Chinese family were unleashed. This insight gains further credence when one compares the case of Hong Kong and other ethnic Chinese overseas communities, on the one hand, with the case of the People's Republic, on the other. And if we are to trust current reports about what is going on today in the PRC's southern provinces, we discover that Chinese entrepreneurial familism is the driving force here as well. What remains to be seen, however, is whether this Chinese entrepreneurial familism will also be able to create the basis for the emergence of stable political structures analogous to those of the West.

Once More: The Western Family Today

These three brief illustrations provide us with some general insights. Contrary to the opinions of many experts, the cases used demonstrate that change does not take place in the society as a whole, but occurs throughout the web of diversified collective life, in the microcosms of families that compose it. For change leading to prosperity and political stability to occur, a particular family structure and a religiously inspired moral charter appear to be indispensable prerequisites. It is here, and not at the planning boards of governments that the syntheses productive of the formation of modern institutions occur. Conversely, we are alerted to the possibility that hopes for the future of already highly modern societies can be destroyed, and even lost, if the basic elements feeding them stagnate, harden, or are driven into the underground. The family imperative which was so instrumental in altering the history of the West, and which today is active in the pending transformation of the slums of Third World cities, as well as in the creation of prosperity among overseas Chinese, applies in equal measure—I would argue—to our highly modern industrial democracies as well.

It is, therefore, of singular importance for us to remember that only the family—and a very specific type at that—can spontaneously produce the social forms necessary for adequately linking autonomous individuals—regardless of ethnicity and social class—to the macro-structures of modern society. This type of family, more than any other, is peculiarly suited for producing self-reliant, morally accountable, and entrepreneurial individuals who become the carriers of political responsibility and economic prosperity. In this the nuclear family in its 'bourgeois' form serves a mediating function between autonomous individuals and the megastructures of society. In this sense I think it legitimate to argue that the fate of the bourgeois family and the fate of our type of society are inexorably intertwined.

It would be the ultimate irony of history if at the very moment when one country after another around the globe begins to discover the salutary role of the bourgeois type of family not only in the formation of their political economy but also in the organization of their social life, the West is losing faith in the legitimacy of the manner of life that has made for its ascendancy. Jon Davies and Allan Carlson, in their fascinating contributions to this volume and Norman Dennis in *Families Without Fatherhood*[7] argue passionately that Western liberal democracies have already gone a long way down the slippery road of atomized individualism. All three are inclined to argue that the 'appetitive individualism' accepting of an endless variety of sexual and procreative relationships, unencumbered by familial and larger social obligations, has bereft the societies of the West of internal stability. In their interpretation, current trends give reason to argue that Western societies are predestined to fall apart from within.

My own interpretation of the available data and understanding of the trends of the past decades, however, lead me to different conclusions. To be sure the phenomenal rise in the rates of divorce, illegitimate births, and abortions are only too real. Women have entered the labour force in unprecedented numbers and clearly will not return to the home. Early childhood socialization will increasingly occur in out-of-home settings. Adolescents are sexually active earlier and mature later. The delinquency rates are sky-rocketing in most Western liberal democracies (though not only there) and while the drug addiction rate for teenagers has somewhat declined, the alcoholism rate is up. At the same time, it should be noted that the increase in the divorce rate has stabilized, the birth rate is up, and the drug addiction and delinquency appear to be concentrated in select groups of the inner cities cross-nationally. Most importantly though, while the young tend to marry on the whole later today, marriage itself appears to be as popular as ever.

Some of the 'root causes' of these significant shifts may undoubtedly be linked to a new kind of 'family pathology' as Allan Carlson argues; others, however, may not. They have their origin in a general loss of nerve of segments of the elites, the irresponsible practices of a politicized and sensationalist media as well as irrevocable changes of long-standing origin (such as technological transformations, shifts in the production order, secularization and the pluralization of life worlds). The war over the family has become a battle between various camps, all equally eager to secure their particular agendas through the kind of government intervention most profess to abhor.

It is remarkable to observe how through all these tumultuous events and commotions the ideal of the individualistic familism of bourgeois provenance has remained largely intact. Why is this so, you may ask? I would suggest that the reasons may be found in the flexibility of this type of family to mediate between deeply ingrained and contradictory human sentiments for individual autonomy on the one hand and exclusive sexual relationships of intensity and duration on the other. At the same time, no other family arrangement seems to be able to provide a better vehicle for an individual's success in education and life beyond while simultaneously providing for its members a 'haven in a heartless world' regardless of race, religion, or social class. And above all, no other family system than the nuclear conjugal family of the rising middle classes, itself the creator of the capitalist revolution, has been better able to put into place realistic opportunities for the realization of the fundamental yearning of all human beings to own and create one's own little world, however differently defined. For the vast majority of ordinary families around the globe it presents a great variety of life styles from which to choose. Following in the footsteps of Friedrich Hayek, we may thus conclude that if some of the life styles people choose should turn out to be destructive, then individuals will have to accept that they will have to pay the costs. While it falls upon governments, elites, and the media to alert people to the possible consequences of their action, the costs should not be hidden under any circumstances. With these thoughts in mind I am willing to enter into a wager: if people have been informed about these consequences, the vast majority would opt for the family pattern discussed in this paper, and not only for utilitarian reasons. For it is the bourgeois family with all its tedium, problems and dangers that is able to respond in some fashion to the deepest yearnings of human beings wherever they may be.

Notes

1   Schama, Simon, *The Embarrassment of Riches*, Cambridge University Press, 1979.

2   Macfarlane, Alan, *The Origins of English Individualism*, Blackwell, 1978; and *The Culture of Capitalism*, Blackwell, 1987.

3   de Soto, Hernando, *The Other Path*, NY: Harper and Row, 1988.

4   Rosen, Bernard, *The Industrial Connection*, NY: Aldine Press, 1982.

5   Martin, David, *Tongues of Fire*, Blackwell, 1990.

6   Gordon Redding, S., *The Spirit of Chinese Capitalism*, Berlin and NY: de Gruyter, 1990.

7   Dennis, N and Erdos, G., *Families Without Fatherhood*, London: IEA Health and Welfare Unit, 1992.

Liberty, Order and the Family

Allan Carlson

Does liberty rest on strong families? Or might strong families impede liberty? Shifting definitions of both terms confuse any answer.

In recent decades, nonetheless, the latter claim has been dominant. Heavily influenced by modern feminist scholarship, but with roots in Hobbes, Locke, Mill and Rousseau, this view has held that the family is an artificial institution which imposes collective goals on free personalities and interferes with the full development of the autonomous individual. For Thomas Hobbes, family relations were merely another exercise in power, where 'dominion over the infant' was claimed by selfish parents and the honour shown to them by children was 'nothing else but the estimation of another's power'.[1]

John Locke managed to carve out 'a sort of rule and jurisdiction' for parents over small children, which could justify a form of marriage. But he anticipated an early emancipation of the young, while the marital bond, its function gone, 'dissolves itself.'[2] In his discussion of the authority of society over the individual, J.S. Mill revealed his distaste for 'social morality,' even when mediated through private means, which subtly recast liberty into the denial of moral convention.[3] Turning specifically to the family structure of mid-19th century England, he labelled it oppressive, the seedbed of despotism, and the source of human misery 'which swells to something appalling.'[4] Writing more recently in a related tradition, John Rawls concluded that the principle of 'fair opportunity' for individuals could never be achieved in a family-based society, given the innate inequalities imposed within families by gender, wealth, and parental ability. 'Is the family to be abolished then? Taken by itself and given a certain primacy, the idea of equal opportunity inclines us in this direction.'[5]

Another philosophical stream has emphasized the liberating power of government, relative to family. Jean Jacques Rousseau cited the role of the state as an instrument for dissolving traditional loyalties, where 'each of us puts his person and all his power under the supreme direction of the general will.' Personal liberty of a sort would be achieved through state agency—the only entity with sufficient power to check the claims of biological origin and the past.[6] Nineteenth century philosopher T.H. Green saw government as the agent of 'positive liberty', through laws giving individuals the freedom to approach 'moral perfection' and delivering basic security.[7] Writing in the last decade, political economists Samuel Bowles and Herbert Gintis pointed to the family as a prime source of oppression, the spawning ground for imperialism, racism, violence, homophobia, and religious intolerance. Human liberty, they argued, might be won only through the victory of individual rights, defined by and mediated through the state.[8]

These are deviations, however, from the correct historic meaning of liberty, paths leading toward libertinism at one extreme and a form of totalitarianism at the other. The original American view of liberty grew out of the older phrase, liberties, understood as the relative absence of coercive, centralized state authority over natural communities such as households and villages, and the individuals sheltered within them. From Aristotle, this perspective held that all human society began through 'a union of those who cannot exist without each other, namely, of male and female, that the race may continue.' From the households so created, the neighbourhood, village, or community would be born. As these drew together, they would cede authority to the incipient state.[9]

American constitutionalism rested on the same chain of social construction.[10] One defender of American liberty, Thomas Jefferson, emphasized the central importance of autonomous families in reconciling order with liberty. Writing to John Jay in 1785 about the American social system, Jefferson declared that republican government depended on free-standing agrarian households. As he explained: 'Cultivators of the earth are the most valuable citizens. They are the most vigorous, the most independent, the most virtuous, and they are tied to their country, and wedded to its liberty and interests, by the most lasting bonds.' Households, so understood, created a viable balance between the individual and the society. They placed limits on private ambition and forced a reconciliation between the individual's quest for wealth and the needs of the community and posterity. With a certain prescience, Jefferson also saw such households, and the liberty they sustained, threatened by two forces. On the one hand, he indicted the spread of industrial manufacture, labelling 'the class of artificers' as 'the instrument by which liberties of a country are overturned.' On the other hand, he feared the growth of the state, noting that '[t]he natural progress of things is for liberty to yield and government to gain ground.'[11] These are themes to which we shall return.

Defined in accordance with this view of liberty, a 'family' is a man and a woman bonded together in a socially-approved covenant of marriage to provide mutual care and protection, to create a small economy of shared production and consumption, to bear, rear, and protect children, and to maintain continuity with the generations which came before and those which shall come in the future. More than an arbitrary choice of categories lies behind this definition. Both the anthropological record and the insights of modern sociobiology suggest that this family structure is, with modest variations, nearly universal among healthy human cultures and probably imprinted in the genetic inheritance of the human species.[12] So understood, the family resolves the false dichotomy between individual freedom and collective social responsibility and creates conditions where ordered liberty can exist.

The modern social problem lies in the rapid unravelling of family life seen in all Western nations during this century, and most vividly in the last thirty years, which has imperiled the prospects for an ordered liberty. My intent is to identify the pressures that have weakened families, to discuss the consequences, and to propose mechanisms that might restore autonomy for families, and so improve the prospects for liberty and social peace in the millennium about to dawn.

The Economic Revolution

The weakening of the family unit can be analyzed through its loss of functions and the consequent decline of the family as a source of sustenance and security and as a focus of loyalty for individuals.

As Jefferson correctly foresaw, two institutions have grown large at the family unit's expense: the industrial economy and the state.

The introduction of machine technology and the factory system of production forced the reordering of Western social life, beginning in the late 18th century. Before their appearance, the daily flow of events for the vast majority of the European peoples had been surprisingly stable. For over a millennium, householding had been the dominant economic pattern. Residence and workplace were normally one and the same, be it in the form of a farmer's cottage or a craftsman's shop. Household production, ranging from toolmaking and weaving to the keeping of livestock and the garden patch, bound each family together as an economic unit, 'a community of work.'[13] Production complemented consumption, and made the family largely self-sufficient, albeit at a relatively mean and sometimes precarious level of existence. Wives and children stood beside husbands and fathers as co-workers in the family enterprise, with no debate over issues of gender roles and dependency.[14] Into the 19th century, markets and money were of limited importance to the average farmer, cottager, or craftsman. In the European countryside, a varied mix of residual feudal obligations, payments-in-kind, barter, and subsistence agriculture predominated.[15] In towns, labour was bound in by an elaborate series of customs and regulations designed, in part, to preserve 'the dignity of workers' and the autonomy of households.

Matters were little different in North America. Challenging the dominant interpretation which has viewed the United States as 'born modern,'[16] a new view of early American social history has emerged over the last twenty-five years. Instead of a land composed of individualistic entrepreneurs and speculators, this America was, until the 1820-60 period, a place characterized by age-stratification and patriarchal power, by strong kin connections and dominant ethnic and religious communities, and by a household mode of production bonded to subsistence agriculture: in short, an America much closer to the hierarchical family systems of Europe than previously supposed.

This interpretation portrays the vast majority of early Americans—roughly 90 per cent—arranging their labour along family lines, where 'family' and 'economy' formed a rough unity, and where family relations were conditioned by economic questions of property and labour. In this family economy, parents enjoyed the legal possession of property—as freeholders, tenants, or share-croppers—and counted their children as workers. In turn, these adults were dependent on their children for economic support in old age and so focused great attention on the terms and timing for transferring economic resources to the succeeding generation.[17]

These Americans also shared an overriding focus on the soil, particularly the preservation of the family freehold into the future. They understood autonomy, and liberty, to rest on the possession of land, and the ability to be self-sufficient. Quaker farmers in the Delaware Valley, as an example, were a community committed to the creation of families through a child-centred use of land, where the family unit served as a revolving fund, shifting land resources between generations over the life cycle. Looking at Andover, Massachusetts, another historian discovered 'the consuming concern' of fathers to be the settlement of their sons upon the land as independent freeholders. Other regional studies from the 1790s have shown that only one fifth of American farms produced a sufficient surplus to engage in any market transactions: the large majority existed in a non-cash system of local exchange based on crude 'just price' theories.[18] In this era, American children were numerous (the average white woman in America, circa 1800, would bear seven live children over her lifetime), while inter-generational bonds were strong.[19] As one historian, looking at the early American Republic, concluded: 'The line was more important than the individual; the patrimony was to be conserved for lineal reasons'[20] —a surprisingly 'European' sentiment.

In both Europe and North America, industrialization and its attendant changes tore the settled, family-oriented world asunder. Day labour for hire replaced family production for self-sufficiency; dependence on market forces supplanted the independence of the household. In historian John Demos' words, 'family life was wrenched apart from the world of work—a veritable sea-change in social history.'[21] The goods produced by factories using the division of labour rapidly displaced family produced commodities such as cloth, shoes, and candles. The unique demands of the new machines, the construction of ever larger factories, and the need for labour discipline further severed the workplace from the home. Among those persons in the new economic order, household living lost most productive functions and the autonomy which went with them, with family units reorganizing as places for shared consumption and shelter. Through legal changes abolishing rural and guild privileges, labour became a commodity governed for the first time by national and international markets. The new economy levelled the reciprocal, complementary tasks of husbands and wives in household production, threw marital partners into competition with each other in the sale of their labour, and raised questions about gender roles in the industrial order. Children over the age of six or seven, too, could trade in the obedience demanded by lineage and birth for the freedom to sell their own labour to the manufacturers. In the industrial environment, the autonomous, cooperative, self-sufficient family changed into a collection of individuals in potential, and often real rivalry. As residual dependents, infants, small children, the sick, and the old had no immediate prospects for individual economic gain; the new market-driven incentives left their fate uncertain.

At least relative to children, the leading political economist of the new order, Adam Smith, envisioned no serious problem so long as their labour and insurance value were family-controlled commodities. As he explained in his *Wealth of Nations*:

> Labour [in North America] is...so well rewarded that a numerous family of children, instead of being a burden, is a source of opulence and prosperity to the parents. The value of children is the greatest of all encouragements to marriage. We cannot, therefore, wonder that the people in North America should generally marry very young.

Indeed, Smith calculated the labour of each child, before it left home, to be worth 'a hundred pounds clear gain' to parents.[22] Nonetheless, he also held that adult labour would be primarily responsible for family support, and borrowed from the Physiocrats the concept of a natural wage. He was aware that a competitive wage market gave no cognizance to family burden: an unmarried worker and a worker supporting a wife and ten children at home would receive, in theory, the same pay for the same work. However, moving from direct observation into a kind of metaphysics, Smith argued that 'parental tenderness' was innate to humans, since the survival of the species depended on it. This led to his conclusion that sentiments of 'common humanity' would ensure delivery of a natural wage commensurate with natural family duties: in other words, the creation through social and cultural sentiments of a family-sustaining wage.[23]

David Ricardo shared this confidence in social wisdom under a regime of economic liberty, provided that government stayed out of the business of fixing wages and providing charity. As he wrote in an 1821 letter:

> If men depended wholly on their own exertions for support, a state of society might and I think would exist, in which it could not be 'successfully shown that no labourer and very few artisans have a prospect of being able to maintain a family.'

He held faith that the unfettered wage market would produce a natural family wage, where:

> [a] man's wages should, and would on a really good system, be sufficient not only to maintain himself and family when he is in full work, but also to enable him to lay up a provision...for those extraordinary calls.[24]

The Aggressor State

The state, though, was not a disinterested actor relative to the family. To the degree that industrialization and its attendant changes—migration, urbanization, rural depopulation—transferred productive functions from families to the market and placed internal stress on family relationships, the abstract state also faced new opportunities for growth by taking functions and power from the family. These changes, over time, subverted the conditions set by Smith and Ricardo for family survival within an industrial economy, forced families to ever greater reliance on outside agencies, and so diminished liberty. The key variable proved to be the parent-child economic bond, the key indicator the birth rate, and the first issue mandatory state education.

Social historians have long viewed fertility change as a prime indicator of relative social stress. John Caldwell's important 1982 volume, *Theory of Fertility Decline*, represents a cross-cultural effort, based on extensive anthropological research, to understand the cause of declining birthrates in the modern world. Caldwell argues that fertility falls only when there is a change in the economic relationships within the family. In traditional societies with a 'familial mode of production,' the flow of wealth is from children to parents. Children exist as economic assets, and fertility is high. However, as the 'labour market mode of production' breaks into a society, the flow of wealth reverses, now going from parents to children.

In an important turn of his argument, Caldwell emphasizes that it is not urbanization or the rise of industry, *per se*, that brings this change in family relations. Rather, it is the prior development, importation, or promulgation of new, individualistic ideas through mass education that causes the critical shift in the parent-child relationship. Educated children, Caldwell explains, expect to be given more and to be demanded of less by their parents, and their economic importance for parents evaporates, or even reverses. State-mandated education, he concludes, serves as the driving force behind the shift in preference from a large to a small family and in the reconstruction of the residual, diminished family as limited and egalitarian, with its members primarily engaged economically outside the home.[25]

In a parallel explanation, Princeton University demographer Norman Ryder places the same stress on the role of mass education as the primary agent in releasing individuals from obligation to kin. 'Education of the junior generation is a subversive influence,' he writes:

> Boys who go to school distinguish between what they learn there and what their fathers can teach them. The reinforcement of the [family] control structure is undermined when the young are trained outside the family for specialized roles in which the father has no competence.

A related struggle goes on between the family and the state for the allegiance of the individual. As Ryder puts it:

> [modern industrial] society has interest in the rational allocation of human resources to serve aggregate economic and political ends, and expresses those interests by substituting individualistic for familistic principles in role assignment. Political organisations, like economic organisations, demand loyalty and attempt to neutralize family particularism. There is a struggle between the family and the state for the minds of the young.

In this contest, he continues, the government school serves as:

The chief instrument for teaching citizenship, in a direct appeal to the children over the heads of their parents.

The school also serves as the medium for communicating a 'state morality' and a 'state mythology' designed to subvert those of families.[26]

Evidence from the United States gives strong support to the Caldwell-Ryder emphasis on mandatory state school attendance laws as the first 'subversive' agent in family decline. The sharp fall in American fertility between 1850 and 1900 has long puzzled social historians, for throughout that period the U.S. remained predominantly rural and absorbed masses of young immigrants, conditions normally associated with a high birthrate.

Following Caldwell, though, demographers speculated that the leadership role of the United States in introducing a mass state education system might explain the change. And indeed, U.S. data from 1871 to 1900 show a remarkably strong negative relationship between the fertility of white women and an index of public school growth developed by L.D. Ayres in 1920. Fertility was inversely related to the average number of days that children attended school in a year, and the percentage of children enrolled. Even among farming families, each additional month that a child spent in school decreased family size by .23 children. Moreover, the U.S. fertility decline began first and was strongest in the Northeast, the section of the country also claiming the earliest development of a comprehensive public education system.[27]

Viewed from the economic angle, mandatory school attendance laws represented the socialization of children's time. What had been a private family matter, counted among the ancient liberties, became a state matter, controlled by government authorities and paid for by taxation. Child Labor Laws in the 1900-37 period, capped in the United States by the federal Fair Labor Standards Act, represented a more complete socialization of children's economic value as workers, spanning the whole day and year, not just the school period. Advocates of these measures were rarely shy about their goals. As one American official, in an article linking both subjects, explained: 'The schools exist primarily for the benefit of the State rather than for the benefit of the individual. The State seeks to make every citizen intelligent and serviceable.'[28]

The operating assumptions were that the state now took precedence over the family in managing children, and that most parents were incapable of knowing or defending their children's interests relative to training and learning, functions that must now pass to the expertise of government. From an alternate perspective, though, Adam Smith's criteria for family survival in the new economic order had suffered a crippling blow.

Another aggressive seizure of family functions came in the 1930s, with passage of the Social Security Act.[29] As in other Western countries, the U.S. central government would provide old-age pensions to the elderly without attention to telling actuarial distinctions, to be paid for by transferring income from current workers to current retirees. From the family's perspective, this single move cut the bonds of economic security between the three generations of a single family. Put another way, 'the insurance value of children' had also now been socialized. One's own children were no longer needed as an investment towards security in later life. Indeed, the 'value' of children had been precisely reversed. In the welfare state, where income and payroll taxes were mandatory, one could *improve* one's immediate standard-of-living, and suffer no long-term negative consequences, by having only one or—even better—no children at all. As Swedish economist Gunnar Myrdal aptly described this new demographic contradiction, in 1940:

> While practically all married people try to limit the number of their children to some extent in order to defend the family standard of living, and while an increasing number carry out this limitation to the extreme, practically no one [now] breeds children as an investment...to secure support in old age.[30]

In America, at least, it took time for the new system rooted in state control to drive out the old one rooted in the liberty of households. As late as 1957, 52.5 per cent of persons age 65 or over still reported receiving some income support from their children, compared to the 41.6 per cent receiving some support from Social Security. As late as 1960, a full 60 per cent of widowed women 75 years and older still lived with relatives, often in a multigenerational family. By 1980, though, a mere four per cent of the elderly received some financial support from children (indeed, the elderly were now twice as likely to report *providing* financial help to grown children rather than receiving it) while the number of aged widows living with relatives had tumbled from 60 to 33 per cent.[31]

Again, these were not so much accidents of history, but intentional appropriations of family functions by state officials guided by an operational theory. In his influential three-volume study, *A Social History of The American Family* (1917), Arthur Calhoun had argued that 'American history consummates the disappearance of the wider familism and the substitution of the parentalism of society.' Concluding that large numbers of natural parents were totally unfit for the task, he said that children in an industrial age of necessity passed 'into the custody of community experts who are qualified to perform the more complex functions of parenthood...which the parents have neither the time nor knowledge to perform'.[32]

The American sociologist William F. Ogburn, in his contribution to the semi-official volume *Recent Social Trends (1934)*, prepared by the Herbert Hoover Administration, emphasized 'the decline of the institutional functions of the family'. The modern family, he noted, no longer produced its own food, shelter, and clothing. 'Religious observances within the home are said to be declining'. Recreation now focused on theatres, dance halls and ball parks. Home baking and canning had disappeared. Married women flowed into the workplace. Care and protection of the old passed over to public agency. The public school teacher served 'as a substitute parent in regard to the function of training the child'. Even the 'personality' and 'emotional' tasks of the family, seen by some theorists as the last functions left to the home, were failing, as educational and social changes widened the gap between the generations. In sum, the family unit and the sense of liberty it had sustained were archaic, and doomed.[33]

The state's acquisition of power to the disadvantage of family occurred in other ways, as well. For example, female opponents of women's suffrage claimed that extending the vote to women would politicise marriages, accentuate individualism at the expense of family solidarity, and elevate politics and state control to the disadvantage of household autonomy and the liberty it sheltered. As an historian of the anti-suffrage movement explains, the root assumption of these women was Aristotelian:

> A primary assumption of the Antis was that the family was the basic nexus, the self-governing unit upon which the state was built. Therefore, as a microcosm of the state, every well-regulated family had to have one head, for if authority were divided the outcome would be domestic anarchy.[34]

A direct assault on household integrity by agents of the state came under the guise of 'child saving'. Born in America through the Reform School Movement of the 1830s, this effort to 'save' children from 'inadequate' parents grew rapidly. An 1839 Pennsylvania Supreme Court decision blessed the campaign by crafting an argument, twisted from England's Chancery laws, based on *parens patriae*, or 'parenthood of the state'. As the justices explained:

> May not the natural parents, when unequal to the task of education or unworthy of it, be supplanted by the *parens patriae*, or common guardianship of the community?[35]

Going beyond cases of real and serious abuse, the *parens patriae* doctrine and its phalanx of agents quickly evolved into a mechanism for social control, a knifethrust into the very heart of family autonomy. Early social workers were commonly the childless offspring of the Anglo-Saxon elite; Irish and Italian families were the frequent objects of their intervention. Children of 'the poor' and of 'foreigners' were institutionalized without respect for *habeas corpus* and other aspects of due process. Affected parents found themselves nearly helpless, unable to protect their children from seizure by state agents. At best, affected families survived only as they submitted to *de facto* service as agents of the state themselves, acknowledging this cession of their children and their liberty.

Between 1899 and 1920, the Juvenile Court Movement spread across the land. Its most faithful propagandist, Miriam Van Waters, argued in her aptly titled book, *Parents on Probation*, that 'hardly a family in America is not engaging in the same practices, falling into the same attitudes, committing the same blunders which...bring the court families to catastrophe'. Parents could no longer 'shield themselves behind *natural* rights', she said. It was 'only a question of time before the parent's psychological handling of his child' would also be subject to state scrutiny. In the future, she proclaimed, *every* parent would be brought into the therapeutic arms of state social work, 'willingly cooperate in a plan for his own welfare', and then face 'the superparent, which is mankind', with a 'face stained with tears', saying: 'Sure, I'll make good'.[36]

The contemporary campaign against child abuse is the direct descendant of these sentiments, a coercive state effort that is disrupting, and sometimes destroying, hundreds of thousands of innocent American families each year. Where real incidents of child abuse are probably increasing as a consequence of a growing number of children in broken families (to which I will return later), the broader effort is in the Van Waters spirit. Hysteria bound to professional self interest has brought a new surge of state intervention into families, where the Common Law's view of the home as inviolable has been forgotten.[37] The related campaign for 'children's rights' has offered state agents still greater opportunities to pry apart the residual loyalties of family members to each other.[38]

The abstract state has also used 'divorce reform', in recent years, to undermine marriage and so diminish natural liberty. In historic and secular terms, marriage in the Western world represented a social covenant between a man and a woman, who agreed to provide each other a basic level of mutual care, 'for richer, for poorer, for better, for worse, in sickness or in health'. In other words, if trouble or tragedy struck one partner, the marriage vow guaranteed to the community that the other partner would not abandon his or her spouse. Similarly, marriage was an agreement between the couple and the community, allowing the former to beget and rear children in a manner that would provide the offspring basic levels of nurture and support. The moral basis of the state's intervention into marriage lay in this presumed commitment to family stability for socially constructive ends.

America's 'no fault' divorce revolution of the 1960s and 1970s left marriage vows with a legal force less than that of the weakest contract at will. (Great Britain's 1969 Divorce Reform Act and subsequent changes appear to have had a similar effect.) By granting a divorce at the petition of only one partner, the state has now allied itself with spouses seeking to break the marital contract. As sociologist Lenore Weitzman explains, 'No fault [divorce] is redefining marriage as a time-limited, contingent arrangement rather than a lifelong commitment'. Another legal scholar asks:

If the assumption is that a marriage will end in divorce, why should any party take any selfless action? And, in fact, why should the party with the most to lose from divorce ever contemplate entering this formerly holy and eternal union at all?'[39]

By elevating one partner's right-to-divorce over the other partner's right-to-stay-married, the state has also transformed the rules for marriage to the advantage of government growth. As families fail through divorce, and promises to spouse and children are cast aside, human misery grows as do 'needs' requiring government attention. It was G.K. Chesterton who identified 'the trend toward divorce' as an aspect of 'that modern change which would make the state infinitely superior to the family'.[40] Harvard University law professor Mary Ann Glendon makes a related point, seeing an interest for both government and the industrial economy in weakened marriage. As she notes, modern Americans are 'loosely held in their families, closely bound to occupational or government-derived statuses'.[41]

Social and cultural attempts to employ the sentiments of 'common humanity' (Adam Smith) to construct 'a really good system' (David Ricardo) delivering a family-sustaining wage also faced state assault in the mid 20th century. For over a century, social theorists had sought to build a family wage economy. The common thread was the effort to limit family employment in the industrial economy to a single adult, normally the father, as a means of protecting the household's integrity and independence. In Europe, this usually evolved into a state system of family allowances, as first developed in interwar France. In Australia, it eventually took the form of state-established minimum wages, differentiated by gender.[42] Both developments, however, could be plausibly described as the partial socialization of the child support function, another enhancement of state authority at the expense of family solidarity and liberty.

In America, by way of contrast, the dominant vehicles for delivering a family-sustaining wage were labour contracts (particularly through the work of the American Federation of Labour), voluntary actions by employers (Henry Ford's 1914 programme of paying higher wages to male heads-of-households stands as the best example), and job categories culturally differentiated by gender.[43] All of these mechanisms were free of state coercion and expense, reinforced the autonomous household, and appear to be the kind of developments for which Smith and Ricardo looked.

Starting in 1942, however, the principle of gender equality, mediated through the state, began to take precedence. Federal government orders to war industries that year forced employers to pay equal wages to women for work 'on the same or similar operations'. By 1944, over 2,000 firms with government war contracts reported making adjustments to comply with the order, which gives some indication of the purposeful 'profamily' discrimination in wages that existed in 1941.[44] This measure put an effective end to intentional, large scale wage discrimination in the United States in favour of male head-of-households.

However, the third factor—labour segregation through the cultural maintenance of 'male' and 'female' jobs—quickly more than compensated for this intrusion of government into social wage determination. Between 1939 and 1966, the median wages of women, compared to men, fell from 59.29 per cent to 53.66 per cent. This occurred even though the proportion of females of working age with income rose from 39 per cent in 1947 to 61 per cent in 1966. Part of the explanation lay in the declining proportion of women working 'full time' relative to 'part time'. But the more significant factor was the crowding of women into employment categories that were over 90 per cent female: file clerks; key punch operators; secretaries; typists; and other forms of service work. Meanwhile, women lost ground in 'mens' job categories: attorneys; chemists; engineers; and draughtsmen. Factories, too, became more male: where 26 per cent of all employed women were factory workers in 1947, only 17 per cent were in 1966. Not coincidentally, clerical work and other 'womens jobs' enjoyed the lowest increases in salary over this time span, while chemists, accountants, and other 'male' jobs enjoyed the highest.[45] As late as 1964, the Lyndon Johnson Administration could report to the United Nations that the American wage system rested on the assumption of 'one principal earner' per family. Without any coercion from the state, the marketplace and the sentiments of 'common humanity' had conspired to deliver a rough, natural, family wage to Americans well into the 1960s.

Title VII of the Civil Rights Act of 1964 destroyed this American-made family wage, and undermined the residual household autonomy which it sustained. The measure made it illegal for employers of fifteen or more persons to discriminate against persons in their hiring, firing, or terms of employment due to sex (as well as race, colour, religion, or national origin).[46] For a few years, the measure's impact was unclear. In 1967, though, President Johnson issued Executive Order 11375 to force the pace of change. It prohibited the Federal government and its contractors and subcontractors from discriminating in employment on the basis of sex, and mandated 'affirmative', 'result oriented' measures to eliminate job segregation by sex. In the 1968-71 period, according to a sympathetic commentator, the federal Equal Employment Opportunity Commission (EEOC) 'converted Title VII into a magna carta for female workers, grafting to it a set of rules and regulations that certainly could not have passed Congress in 1964, and perhaps not a decade later, either'.[47] By 1974, EEOC enforcement measures had already narrowed the male/female earnings differential by 14 per cent in the private sector.[48] Framed philosophically, the solution offered by Smith and Ricardo to the market economy's 'family problem' had lost out to the Rawlsian commitment to 'equal opportunity'. Viewed politically, the natural liberty of autonomous households had suffered another blow.

A 'Post-Family' Society?

The pressures of industrialization combined with the self-interested growth of the state have sharply reduced the sphere of the family. A peculiar dialectic has been at work, where family stress caused by industrialization is used to justify intervention by government, which further weakens families, which results in greater social pathology, which justifies further state intervention as the means to reduce disorder. In consequence, the critical functions of the production of goods, the raising and preparation of food, the care and education of the young, and the care and security of the sick and the old have all passed, to a greater or lesser extent, from the family to the mega-institutions of the corporation and the state. The natural family economy, resting on the covenant of marriage and the control over and loyalty of children, has been seriously weakened. As the economic logic of marriage and children has diminished, the state has moved in as care giver and protector to all. And liberty, understood as the relative absence of state authority over natural social communities and the individuals they shelter, has been lost.

While the focus of this discussion has largely been on the United States, the same set of developments are found throughout the North Atlantic region. Rutgers University sociologist David Popenoe, himself a Social Democrat, suggests that the 'welfare state', constructed as a substitute for the family, needs a better label to describe the new level of personal dependence on government. He proposes the phrase, 'client society', to describe nations 'in which citizens are for the most part clients of a large group of public employees who take care of them throughout their lives'.[49]

In the society towards which all Western nations tend, the elderly are free of potential dependence on their grown children; infants, small children, and youth are in some ways free of reliance on their parents for protection and basic support; grown adults are free of meaningful obligations either to their biological parents or to their children; and men and women are free of binding mutual promises in marriage. These freedoms have come in exchange for a kind of universal dependence on the state, the extensive bureaucratization of what had once been family living, and the loss of family autonomy and natural liberty.

The most telling symbol of 'post-family humanity' is the striking rise in the number of people living alone. In Sweden, as example, fully two-thirds of the population of city-centre Stockholm live in single person households. Such units are also the fastest growing component of Great Britain's population, climbing from 12 per cent of all households in 1961 to 26 per cent in 1991, with the fastest growth among persons *under* the 'pensionable age'. In America, the dynamic growth sector has been in 'non-family households', climbing from 7.9 million in 1960 to 27 million in 1989. These are mostly persons living alone, free of all economically draining family bonds and dependent on the employer and the state.

The other dynamic growth sector in Sweden, the United Kingdom, and America is among single women with children. In Sweden, about half of all births are now outside of marriage (although many of these occur in consensual unions). Among British citizens, 28 per cent of births were outside of marriage in 1991, an astonishing increase from 11 per cent in 1979. Among Americans, the figure in 1988 was 26 per cent, although among black Americans the figure rose to 64 per cent. In each country, it seems, women have found that men bound to them in an economically meaningless marriage are no longer necessary. Through job preferment and equal opportunity laws, and through state grants, allowances, housing, and insurance (health and old age) of somewhat varied structure, they find that they can go it alone, through necessity or choice. Two sociologists describe this phenomenon as 'The Mother-State-Child-Family', a social form probably unique to the late 20th century.[50]

Curiously, 'society' still counts on families to function as a moral force, controlling children and the young, and imparting a moral code to the next generation. In the United States, circa 1992, politicians of all ideological persuasions now agree that *only* family reconstruction can save the nation from social disaster,[51] a point reinforced by the Los Angeles riots. But the modern family, where still found, is clearly an institution in decline. Asked to command the attention of children for moral instruction, the average family holds diminishing functional power relative to its two principle rivals, the modern corporation and the modern state. These institutions offer money, security, protection, and power. They confer dignity, social respect, and self worth. They open avenues to control and success. The diminished modern family, in contrast, can offer only a lifetime of principled opposition to the more potent political and economic incentives, tied to moralistic lectures on widely ignored measures of right and wrong to distracted ears. This family still has some claim of love, but all the other tools of potential loyalty have passed or are passing into rival hands. It appears that love is not enough to hold a family together.

Family Decline and Social Pathology
Accordingly, it is tempting simply to write off the diminished modern family as history's loser, the residue of another age, and to accept personal freedom as a substitute for an older conception of liberty. However, if it is true that the family unit is natural, or

innate to the human species, then it cannot be so easily dismissed. In fact, attempts to live in a post-family universe would predictably result in turmoil, with mounting examples of social and personal disorder that governments cannot control or reverse. Viewed in a positive manner, the evidence would show that liberty and social order could only be reconciled through the family restored.

Indeed, these are the generalizations we find when we turn to the vast social science literature on family structure and social pathology. Even in its weakened contemporary condition, the intact, two-parent family committed to survival as a functional institution still performs better than any other variation as an agent for rearing responsible, healthy, adequately-educated children, and as a means of protecting the life, health, and happiness of adults.

Choose the contemporary social pathology, and family disorder—defined as a falling away from the family model offered earlier in this paper—invariably lies at its root. Consider, for example, the linkage of family decline to criminal behaviour. Sociologist Robert Sampson of the University of Illinois, analysing crime in 171 American cities, found that a city's divorce rate was a better predictor of the robbery rate than were measures of arrest and the severity of sentencing. In a parallel study using British data, he found not only that single-parent households are more likely targets for crime, but also that the neighbours of single-parent households are more likely to be affected by crime than the neighbours of two-parent households.[52] A study of 11,000 urban residents of Missouri, Florida, and upstate New York found that 'the percentage of single-parent households with children between the ages of 12 and 20 is significantly associated with rates of violent crime and burglary'.[53]

A family's growing absorption into the industrial economy—an indicator of lost economic self-sufficiency seen most recently in the movement of mothers into the paid labour force—is also positively linked to crime. University of Toronto sociologists found high rates of delinquency among female teens in both single-parent households and in those where the mother was employed in a career or management position. Indeed, maternal employment has shown up consistently as a link to higher delinquency and juvenile crime. One team of scholars cited 'unsuitable supervision of boy by mother' as a prime cause of delinquency. Criminologist Roger Thompson holds that a primary reason that young boys join gangs is that both parents work, 'and if they didn't have the gang, they'd just have an empty home'.[54]

After a time, family pathology begins to feed on itself. Young male lawbreakers, it appears, grow even more troublesome after fathering illegitimate children.[55] Similarly, a 1988 study conducted at the University of Wisconsin found that daughters raised in single-parent households were far more likely to grow dependent on government welfare than daughters of two-parent households, again intensifying the basis of the pathology.[56] The research work consistently shows, moreover, that race, class, and income status are *not* significant variables in predicting criminal behaviour. Family structure and internal family economics are the keys.[57]

The incidence of suicide also shows a strong relationship to family decline. One hundred years ago, sociologist Emile Durkheim argued that religious belief, communitarian values, and family integrity protected individuals from suicide, while non-belief, individualism, and family break-up left persons vulnerable.[58] Modern data consistently reinforce his insight. One recent review of county and state data in the United States, from 1933 to 1980, found that areas with the highest suicide rates were also the areas with the highest divorce rates, while those regions with very low suicide rates were also the areas with the highest rates of church membership.[59] A similar study clarified that it was not religion, *per se*, that resulted in a lower suicide rate, but the lower *divorce* rate delivered by religious belief.[60] Indeed, the American data causally linking adult suicide to divorce is enormous.[61]

Sociologist Steven Stack has also identified 'domestic individualism', seen in the accelerated turn of wives and mothers from the home economy to the market economy, as a causal factor in driving up the suicide rates of other family members. Concerning husbands, he concludes:

> many working class males, the social class most likely to commit suicide, report that their working wives are becoming too independent and that they no longer feel like 'kings' of the roost...Husbands also find that their working wives have less time to act as their counsellors comforting them from the vicissitudes of life.[62]

Combined with divorce and church attendance variables, Stack found that the labour force participation rate of mothers had an 'unusually strong' direct relationship to the suicide of children.[63]

Other recent work suggests: a strong relationship between the suicide of young men and both the illegitimate birth rate and the proportion of persons living alone,[64] and a causal link between absent fathers and suicidal daughters.[65] Moreover, these relationships hold for nations throughout the Western world. In detailed investigations, for example, Stack has found that divorce in Norway[66] and Denmark[67] also has a high correlation with self slaughter, indicating even in highly advanced welfare states 'the importance of stable marriage and family institutions in suicide prevention'. Data from Scotland, Greece, Canada, England, France, Sweden, Italy, and Spain drive home the same point: as families fail to form, as marriages dissolve, and as families merge more completely into the industrial economy, the suicide rates of both adults and children climb.[68]

The research on drug abuse drives toward similar conclusions. Among early work on heroin addiction, Eva Rosenfeld found that affected families were characterized by father absence through death, divorce, or desertion, and by 'immature mothers'.[69] Nathan Sedin of the National Institutes of Mental Health (NIMH) emphasized the crucial role played by family stress in the creation of an addict:

> the father is detached and uninvolved while the mother, who dominates the family, is...emotionally immature, conflicted, and ambivalent about her family role.[70]

In the comprehensive *The Road To H* by Isador Chein and his team, family relations proved to be the key: a full 97 per cent of 'addict families' showed a 'disturbed relationship' between the parents, compared to 41 per cent in the control group.[71] Using British data from 1966-68, Peter Noble found that the presence of a step-parent in a home doubled the likelihood of narcotic use by girls, when compared to the control group.[72] A nine year (1955-64) study of addicts by William Westley and Nathan Epstein found 'a direct relationship' between the emotional well being of children and the bonding of parents. 'Father-led' families produced 'predominately emotionally healthy children', while 'mother-dominated' families spawned serious pathologies. Equally troubling for children were 'sharing families', where fathers and mothers sought equality. The researchers concluded:

> The acceptance of [traditional] spouse roles correlates with the emotional health of the children.[73]

This research period was capped by the 1972 volume, *Horatio Alger's Children*, developed by Richard Blum and Associates. Among the white, middle-class families studied in the volume, certain qualities were found to be significantly related to the 'low risk' of drug use by children, including a belief in God, regular church attendance, a father-led, authoritative structure, subordination of personal autonomy to self-identification with the family group, mothers more interested in home life, and a deep bond to family tradition, where 'the strength, love, and sometimes glory of father is presented as a reflection of the father before him'. In contrast, families with children at 'high risk' of drug abuse had mothers with hobbies such as auto mechanics and competitive athletics, a higher average level of education and income, a scepticism about God and a low level of religious affiliation, 'high levels of activities that take the mother outside the home', and fathers who were 'overly intellectual, [and] took on mother's functions'.[74]

In more recent work, Denise Kandel has linked marijuana use to 'unconventionality' in mothers and lack of maternal involvement in activities with their children, commonly due to outside employment.[75] A study by Brook, Whiteman, and Gordon found that adolescents who had 'affectionate maternal relations', who were 'conventional', and who had strict traditional fathers were significantly less likely to use illicit drugs.[76] Two studies by Kazuo Yamaguchi and Kandel have even shown that individual steps toward construction of a traditional family unit (e.g., entry into marriage, the birth of a child, or greater gender role differentiation with the mother refocusing on tasks in the home) will cause reduced drug use.[77] In short, the research evidence shows that families which manage to maintain or regain some attributes of a pre-modern household are better able to protect their members from illegal drugs.

Children of high educational attainment claim similar qualities in their families of origin. Sociologists C.E. Bowerman and G.H. Elder Jr., discovered that boys, ages 13-18, who were high achievers had fathers who were the most powerful individual in their family; low achievers were more likely to cite their mothers.[78] A study of 11-year-old boys in England found that father dominance within families was positively correlated with the verbal ability of boys on a standard achievement test.[79] Considerable evidence suggests that fathers have a particular role in imparting gender-specific behaviour to both boys and girls, which is tied, in turn, to improved learning.[80] Paternal headship, same-sex identification of children with parents, maternal nurturing, and a division of labour within the home were all positively linked to children's academic achievement. Moreover, there is mounting evidence that such gender identification is 'natural', an expression of innate genetic imprints that characterize the human species.[81]

Looking at learning from the negative side, there is a large literature linking father-absence to 'dramatic' depressive effects on children.[82] Life in the female-headed household takes on an oppressive cast:

> The mother...does not appear to have the time, energy or orientation to establish a stable and supportive family atmosphere for the adolescent child. Pressed by external circumstances, the mother...seems able to invoke only minimal standards for family survival: unembellished practicality is emphasized, the house is not kept up, there is little cultural richness in the surroundings. Ever present is a sense that the mother is close to being overwhelmed, and her child knows this.[83]

The movement of *both* parents into the labour market also undercuts children's educational achievement. The research shows that children who are placed first in their parents' allocation of time and attention show superior academic skills, compared to children receiving less attention. Quantity of time, not its quality, appears to be the central variable. Relative to verbal achievement, for example, it is not selective training in skills, but a close, time-intensive, ongoing relationship between mother and child which is critical.[84]

While the issue remains hotly contested, there is considerable evidence showing that mothers not in the paid labour force have children with higher cognitive abilities and academic achievement, as compared to working mothers with children. Echoing earlier work, a 1978 study found that the 10-year-old sons of employed, middle-class mothers had lower scores on language and mathematics achievement tests than did the sons of full-time mothers.[85] More recently, sociologists Martha Hill and Greg Duncan, looking at the long-term effects of mother presence in the home, concluded:

> Everything else equal, having a mother employed full-time as opposed to not at all was associated with a half-year less completed schooling and 14 per cent lower wages.[86]

Utilizing the University of Michigan's massive 1975-76 time-use survey and a subsequent 1981-82 interview series, economist Frank Stafford reported 'a significant trade off between a market career and a home career for women'. Among both boys and girls, a mother's market time has a significant negative relationship to teachers' ratings of children's comprehension, concentration, retention skills, language, and ability to work independently.[87] Family integrity, gender differentiation, and residual commitment to home production are, once again, the keys to children's success.

Analysis of still other current social pathologies drives home the critical importance of the intact family and the enormous social price exacted by a growing number of divorced or mother-headed families. Turning to child abuse, for example, David G. Gil observes that:

> The data... suggest an association between physical abuse of children and deviance from normative family structure, which seems especially strong for non-white children.

An investigation of 214 parents of battered babies in Britain found that they 'are likely to be reared in broken homes', with pre-marital pregnancy, illegitimacy, and absence of the child's father among the most common 'precursors of baby battering'. Even remarriage seems unable to help. A research team at McMaster University established in 1985 that:

> preschoolers living with one natural and one step-parent were *40 times* more likely to become child abuse cases than were like-aged children living with two natural parents.

Making the point a different way, in 1985 a NIMH study found that violence against children is actually *decreasing* in America's intact families.[88]

52

To Strengthen Families

Nonetheless, the number of such families is falling in the United States, both relatively and in absolute terms. The economic incentives and political pressures have made it ever more difficult for such families to function, and fewer adults are able to sustain the effort. The consequence is the swelling level of the predictable social pathologies reported in the media: criminal behaviour; adult and juvenile suicide; drug abuse; poor educational achievement; the physical abuse of children; and the breakdown of urban civility.

One contemporary response to family break-up has been to argue for a series of 'helps' and 'supports' to female-headed families designed to restore them to a functional level. 'Father absence *per se*', it is said, is not the question. Rather, if these families only had extra income, more parental contact, male role models, and the means of stronger discipline, then all would be set right.[89] It is no coincidence, though, that this list of needs sounds suspiciously like the traditional role definition of a father, with this difference: programmatic 'compensations' of the sort called for (even if the work) come at a large and very public price; real fathers cost the taxpayers nothing. Indeed, this argument for 'helps' works, in practice, as an argument for an ever-growing state, which can only further diminish residual family bonds.

Another contemporary response is that new family forms, such as cohabitation without marriage, are filling the breech as better adaptations to the demands of modernity. However, the claims made for cohabitation—the one 'new family form' growing rapidly—are failing to materialize. Rather than making for secure relationships, the break-up rate of cohabiting couples is extremely high. Even among cohabiting couples which marry, their divorce rate over ten years ran one-third higher than among American couples who had never cohabited.[90] Rather than a test run securing later happiness,

> cohabitation is related to lower levels of marital interaction, [and] higher levels of marital disagreement and marital instability.[91]

Rather than living free of marriage-imposed spousal abuse, cohabiting women are nearly five times as likely to suffer 'severe violence' as married women.[92] While illegitimacy is rising generally, cohabitating couples actually hold negative attitudes toward children: fewer than one-fifth of them are 'planning for children in the future'.[93] The root problem, it appears, is that cohabitation rests on the refusal to make a commitment to the mutual care and shared resources of a family, which in turn generates the expectation that 'family-like' relationships are temporary, and so unworthy of the investment of time and energy. No society can survive on such a frail base.

The logic of this paper leads instead toward a different response: what might be called the restoration of a regime of liberty. If families are to deliver the protection against social pathologies that only they can provide, then families must be allowed to become more powerful, relative to their modern rivals in the industrial economy and the state. Families can be strengthened in this way only as they are allowed to reclaim some of the functions they have lost.

Except among spiritually dedicated communities such as the Amish in America, industrialization cannot be undone. However, we do have it in our power to allow the natural compensations of a market system to work again. To do this, the politically-imposed disincentives to family living need to be repealed. The agenda following from this analysis includes:

- the dismantling of governmental efforts aimed at gender-role engineering (meaning in the U.S. the elimination of the word sex from Title VII of the Civil Rights Act of 1964 and the repeal of Executive Order 11375), leaving men and women free to reconstitute a natural, family-sustaining wage through the interaction of the common sentiments of humanity;

- divorce law reforms that at least restore the sanctity-of-contract for marriage (meaning, in the United States, the undoing of the 'no fault' divorce revolution);

- a prudent reduction and reform of the state's child protection system, restoring the preference given to the natural rights of parents;

- and the dismantling of federal, state and local restrictions on economic activities in the home, actions ranging from a sharp loosening of zoning requirements and mortgage qualifications to

54

the repeal of portions of the Fair Labor Standards Act and related statutes, which would allow for some physical reintegration of home life with market labour.

Through these actions, families in a free society would have greater opportunity to take control over their destinies. Examples found in the last 150 years—from the informal family wage to the modern home school—testify that negative market incentives affecting families can be controlled, through social convention and human will, provided that individuals understand the problem, keep government out of the way, and have the character to make the effort. With access to more institutional power, this means that parents as family leaders need be willing to assume more real responsibilities for each other, for their children, and for the generations to come. For if ordered liberty is the gift of strong families, these families in turn rest on individual self-governance: on persons who understand their duties and who act in accord with the virtues of fidelity, courage, continence, and reverence.

Notes

1 Hobbes, Thomas, *De Cive: The English Version*, Oxford: Clarendon Press, 1983, pp. 42-48, 122-24.

2 John Locke, *Of Civil Government (Second Essay)*, Ann Arbor, MI: Edwards Brothers, 1947, PP. 35-37, 41-44, 51-54.

3 John Stuart Mill, *On Liberty*, Harmondsworth: Penguin Books, 1986, pp. 141-62.

4 John Stuart Mill, *The Subjection of Women*, Cambridge, MA: The M.I.T. Press, 1970, pp. 22, 28-29, 36-37, 48.

5 John Rawls, *A Theory of Justice*, Cambridge, MA: The Belknap Press of Harvard University, 1971, pp. 74, 301, 462-63, 511.

6 Jean Jacques Rousseau, *The Social Contract*, New York: E.P. Dutton, 1950, pp. 4-5, 15, 27.

7 Green, T.H., *Prolegomena To Ethics*, Oxford: Clarendon Press, 1883, Book I, Chap, 3; and Book II, Chap. 1. On Green's influence in changing the meaning of liberty, see: Fleming, Thomas, 'Unholy Dying', *Chronicles* 16, February 1992: 10-13.

8 Bowles, Samuel and Gintis, Herbert, *Democracy and Capitalism: Property, Community and the Contradictions of Modern Social Thought*, New York: Basic Books, 1986, pp. 4-20, 178-79, 193-95.

9   Aristotle, *Politics, I* 1252a-1263b; 1261a-1263b.

10 I develop this argument more completely in: Carlson, Allan, 'The Family and the Constitution', in *American Federalism: Essays on the Constitution*, (ed) McLean, Edward, B., Lanham, MD: University Press of America, forthcoming.

11 Letters, Thomas Jefferson to John Jay, 23 August 1785; Jefferson to James Madison, 20 December 1787; and Jefferson to Colonel Carrington, 27 May 1788; in *The Life and Selected Writings of Thomas Jefferson*, Koch, Adrienne and Peden, William, (eds), New York: The Modern Library, 1944, 1972, pp. 377, 440-41, 447.

12 This is the provocative argument found in Fleming, Thomas, *The Politics of Human Nature*, New Brunswick, NJ: Transaction Books, 1987, Chapters 4 and 5.

13 Demos, John, *Past, Present, and Personal: The Family and the Life Course in American History*, New York: Oxford University Press, 1968, p. 28.

14 Pinchbeck, Ivy, *Women Workers and the Industrial Revolution, 1750-1850*, London: George Routledge and Sons, 1930, pp. 7-26.

15 See: Slicher van Bath, Heinrich, *The Agrarian History of Western Europe, A.D. 500-1850*, trans. Olive Ordish, London: Edward Arnold, 1963.

16 Found, for example, in: Bailyn, Bernard, *Education in the Forming of American Society: Needs and Opportunity for Study*, Chapel Hill: University of North Carolina Press, 1960, pp. 15-36; Grant, Charles S., *Democracy in the Connecticut Frontier Town of Kent*, New York: Norton, 1961, pp. 53-54, 170-171; and Fliegelman, Jay, *Prodigals and Pilgrims: The American Revolution against Patriarchal Authority, 1750-1800*, Cambridge: Cambridge University Press, 1982, pp. 5-6, 263-67.

17 See: Henretta, James, 'Families and Farms: Mentality in Pre-Industrial America', *William and Mary Quarterly 35*, January 1978: 20-21; Gunderson, Joan R. and Victor Gampel, Gwen, 'Married Women's Legal Status in Eighteenth-Century New York and Virgina,' *William and Mary Quarterly 39*, January 1982: 127-29; Blake Smith, Daniel, 'The Study of the Family in Early America: Trends, Problems and Prospects,' *William and Mary Quarterly 39*, January 1982: 15, 24; and Clark, Christopher, 'Household Economy, Market Exchange, and the Rise of Capitalism in the Connecticut Valley, 1800-1860,' *Journal of Social History 13*, 1979: 169-90.

18 Levy, Barry, '"Tender Plants": Quaker Farmers and Children in the Delaware Valley, 1681-1735,' *Journal of Family History 3*, Summer 1978: 116-29; Greven Jr., Philip, *Four Generations: Population, Land, and Family in Colonial Andover, Massachusetts*, Ithaca, NY: Cornell University Press, 1970, p. 251; Snydacker, Daniel, 'Kinship and Community in Rural Pennsylvania', *Journal of Interdisciplinary History 13*, Summer 1982: 41-61; and Henretta, 'Families and Farms,' pp. 9, 12-15, 18-19, 28-29.

19 Coale, Ansley J. and Zelnick, Melvin, *New Estimates of Fertility and Population in the United States*, Princeton, NJ: Princeton University Press, 1963; and Folbre, Nancy R., 'The Wealth of Patriarchs: Deerfield, Massachusetts, 1760-1840,' *Journal of Interdisciplinary History 16*, Autumn 1985: 217-19.

56

20 Henretta, 'Families and Farms,' p. 26.

21 Demos, *Past, Present, and Personal*, p. 32.

22 Smith, Adam, *An Inquiry into the Nature and Causes of the Wealth of Nations*, (ed) Bullock, C.J., New York: P.F. Collier and Sons, 1903, p. 74-75.

23 Smith, *op. cit.*, pp. 71-75, 84; and Smith, Adam, *The Theory of Moral Sentiments*, New Rochelle, NY: Arlington House, 1969, pp. 195, 321.

24 Letters, Ricardo to Trower, 26 January 1818; and Ricardo to Place, 9 September 1821; quoted in Hollander, Samuel, *The Economics of David Ricardo*, Toronto and Buffalo: University of Toronto Press, 1979, pp. 77, 581.

25 Caldwell, John C., *Theory of Fertility Decline*, New York: Academic Press, 1982, particularly chapters 4 and 10.

26 Ryder, Norman, 'Fertility and Family Structure', *Population Bulletin of the United Nations 15*, 1983: 20-32.

27 Guest, Avery M., Tolnay, Stewart E., 'Children's Roles and Fertility: Late Nineteenth Century United States,' *Social Science and History 7*, 1983: 355-80.

28 Hand, W.H., 'The Need for Compulsory Education in the South', *The Child Labor Bulletin 1*, June 1912: 79. A fascinating discussion of the child labour issue, and its relationship to family strength and liberty, is: Kaufmann, Bill, 'The Child Labor Amendment Debate of the 1920s, or Catholics and Mugwumps and Farmers', paper presented for the Liberty Fund conference, 'Home Production and Liberty', held in Rockford, Illinois, June 1991.

29 According to historian W. Andrew Achenbaum, only the general crisis of the Great Depression was sufficient to break down widespread American distrust of centralized state old-age pensions. In its absence, he suggests that the pressure for change, circa 1928, was simply not strong enough to overcome American traditions of family integrity and personal responsibility. See: Achenbaum, W. Andrew, *Old Age in the New Land: The American Experience since 1790*, Baltimore: The John Hopkins University Press, 1978, pp. 127-28.

30 Myrdal, Gunnar, *Population: A Problem for Democracy*, Cambridge MA: Harvard University Press, 1940, pp. 197-200.

31 Heclo, Hugh, 'The Political Foundations of Anti-Poverty Policy', Paper presented at the conference, 'Poverty and Policy:Retrospect and Prospects', sponsored by the U.S. Department of Health and Human Services, 6-8 December 1984, p. 27; Crystal, Stephen, *America's Old Age Crisis*, New York: Basic Books, 1982, pp. 16-18, 32-37.

32 Calhoun, Arthur W., *A Social History of the American Family: From Colonial Times to the Present*, vol. III, New York: Barnes and Noble, 1945 (1917), pp. 165-75.

33 Ogburn, William F., 'The Family and Its Functions', in The President's Research Committee on Social Trends, *Recent Social Trends in the United States*, Vol.I, New York and London: McGraw-Hill, 1983 [1934], pp. 51, 53-55. Also see Ogburn, *American Marriage and Family Relationships*, New York: Henry Holt, 1928.

34 Camhi, Jane Jerome, 'Women Against Women: American Antisuffragism, 1880-1920', Doctoral dissertation, Tufts University, 1973, p. 9.

35 *Ex Parte Crouse*, 4 Wharton Pa.9, 1838.

36 Van Waters, Miriam, *Parents on Probation*, New York: New Republic, 1927, pp. 3-6, 35, 167. Also: Mack, Julian, 'The Juvenile Court', *Harvard Law Review 23*, 1909: 104. On this general question, see: Platt, Anthony M., *The Child Savers: The Invention of Delinquency*, Chicago: University of Chicago Press, 1969.

37 See: Carlson, Allan, *Family Questions: Reflections on the American Social Crisis*, New Brunswick, NJ: Transaction Books, 1988, Chapter 17 ('Child Savers and the Therapeutic State'). Also: Besharov, Douglas, *Recognizing Child Abuse: A Guide for the Concerned*, New York: The Free Press, 1990.

38 See: Donohue, William A., 'Children's Rights', *The Family in America 2*, November 1988, pp. 1-8.

39 Weitzman, Lenore, 'The Divorce Law Revolution and the Transformation of Legal Marriage', in *Contemporary Marriage: Comparative Perspectives on a Changing Institution*, (ed) Davis, Kingsley, New York: Russell Sage, 1985, pp. 305, 335; and Leiber Presser, Arlynn, 'Divorce, American Style', review of *Divorce Reform at the Crossroads*, (ed) Hill Kay, Herma, and Sugarman, Stephen D., *ABA Journal*, April 1991: 124-25.

40 Chesterton, G.K., *Divorce vs Democracy* (1916), in *Collected Works*,(ed) Marlin, George *et al*, San Francisco: Ignatius Press, 1987, 4:44.

41 Glendon, Mary Ann, *The New Family and the New Property*, Toronto: Butterworths, 1976, p. 227.

42 Rathbone, Eleanor F., *The Case for Family Allowances*, Harmondsworth: Penguin Books, 1940; Pinte, Jean, *Les Allocations Familiales—Origines Regime Legal*, Paris: Librarie de Recueil Siney, 1935; and Anderson, George, *Fixation of Wages in Australia*, Melbourne, Australia: Melbourne University Press, 1929, pp. 188-217.

43 See: Boyle, James, *The Minimum Wage and Syndicalism*, Cincinnati: Stewart and Kidd Co., 1913; May, Martha, 'The Historical Problem of the Family Wage: The Ford Motor Company and the Five Dollar Day', *Feminist Studies 8*, Summer 1978: 401-02; and Ford, Henry, in collaboration with Crawther, Samuel, *My Life and Work*, Garden City, NY: Doubleday, Page & Co., 1922, pp. 116-23.

44 Foner, Philip S., *Women and the American Labor Movement: From World War I to the Present*, New York: The Free Press, 1980, pp. 348-54.

45 See: Clover, Vernon T., *Changes in Differences in Earnings and Occupational Status of Men and Women*, 1947-1967, n.p.: Department of Economics and Business Administration, Texas Tech University, 1970, pp. 4, 17-21, 26-27, 36, 43, 50-51.

46 The inclusion of the word 'sex' in the 1964 legislation actually occurred as a sort of joke. The measure proposed by President Lyndon Johnson did not include gender in its list of illegal discriminations. During debate on the measure in the U.S. House of Representatives, 'Dixiecrat' Howard Smith offered an amendment to add 'sex' to the list. Most observers believe that his strategy was to load the

bill with enough confused and uncertain terms so as to kill it. When his colleagues greeted the amendment with gales of laughter, he assured them that he was 'serious about this thing'. After faltering debate, the amendment was adopted. Significantly, no hearings were held to gauge the effect of this substantial shift in the measure's purpose and coverage. The amendment survived a conference with the Senate, which also never debated the issue or purpose of placing sex in Title VII, and it became law. See Buckley, J.E., 'Equal Pay in America', in Pettman, Barrie O., (ed), *Equal Pay for Women: Progress and Problems in Seven Countries*, Bradford, England: MCB Books, 1975, pp. 45-46.

47 Allen Robinson, Donald, 'Two Movements in Pursuit of Equal Employment Opportunity', *Signs: Journal of Women in Culture and Society 4*, No. 3, 1979: 427.

48 Beller, Andrea, 'Title VII and the Male/Female Earnings Gap: An Economic Analysis', *Harvard Women's Law Journal 1*, 1978: 157-73.

49 Popenoe, David, *Disturbing the Nest: Family Change and Decline in Modern Societies*, New York: Aldine de Gruyter, 1988.

50 Day, Randal D. and Mackey, Wade C.,'The Mother-State-Child "Family": Cul-De-Sac or Path to the Future?', *The Family in America*, March 1988,: 1-8.

51 This was the consensus reached by leading liberals and conservatives in the 1991 final report of The National Commission on Children. See: *Beyond Rhetoric: A New American Agenda for Children and Families, Final Report of the National Commission on Children*, Washington, DC: U.S. Government Printing Office, 1991.

52 Sampson, Robert J., 'Crime in Cities: The Effects of Formal and Informal Social Control', in *Communities and Crime*, (eds), Reiss Jr., Albert J. and Tonry, Michael, vol. 8, in *Crime and Justice*, (eds), Tonry, Michael and Morris, Norvel, Chicago: University of Chicago Press, 1987, pp. 271-307; and Sampson, Robert J., 'Does an Intact Family Reduce Burglary Risks for Its Neighbors?', *Sociology and Social Research 71*, April 1987: 204-07. In this discussion of family life and crime, I need to acknowledge the work of Bryce Christensen in identifying and interpreting the research data through the monthly periodical, *The Family in America* and its 'New Research' supplement.

53 Smith, Douglas A. and Jarjoura, G. Roger, 'Social Structure and Criminal Victimization', *Journal of Research in Crime and Delinquency 25*, February 1988: 27-52.

54 Hagen, John *et al.*, 'Class in the Household: A Power-Control Theory of Gender and Delinquency', *American Journal of Sociology 92* , 1987: 812-14; Glueck, Sheldon and Glueck, Eleanor, *Family Environment and Delinquency*, Boston: Houghton Mifflin, 1962, p. 221; Tompson cited by Clark, Paul, 'Youth Gangs Prone to "Incomprehensible" Violence, UT Professor Says', *Asheville Citizen 13*, October 1988, p. 6A; and Ianni, Francis A.J., *The Search for Structure: A Report on American Youth Today*, New York: Free Press, 1989, pp. 175-210.

55 Pirog-Good, Maureen A., 'Teenage Paternity, Child Support and Crime', *Social Science Quarterly 69*, 1988: 527-47.

56 McLanahan, Sara S., 'Family Structure and Dependency: Early Transitions to Female Household Headship', *Demography 25*, 1988: 1-16.

57 See: Sampson, Robert J., 'Urban Black Violence: The Effect of Male Joblessness and Family Disruption', *American Journal of Sociology 93*, 1983: 348-82; Matsueda, Ross L., and Heimer, Karen, 'Race, Family Structure, and Delinquency: A Test of Differential Association and Social Control Theories', *American Sociological Review 52*, 1987: 826-40; and Schoen, Robert and Kluegel, James R., 'The Widening Gap in Black and White Marriage Rates: The Impact of Population Composition and Differential Marriage Propensities', *American Sociological Review 53*, 1988: 895-907.

58 Durkheim, Emile,*Suicide: A Study in Sociology*, trans. Spaulding, John A. and Simpson, George, Glencoe, IL: The Free Press of Glencoe, 1951, particularly pp.209-210, 253-58, 270-71, 312.
    On this general question, see chapter 18, 'Youth Suicide and the Fate of a Nation', Carlson, *Family Questions*.

59 Breault, K.D., 'Suicide in America: The test of Durkheim's Theory of Religious and Family Integration, 1933-1980', *American Journal of Sociology 92*, November 1986, pp. 651-52.

60 Lester, David, 'Religion, Suicide, and Homicide, *Social Psychiatry 22*, 1987: 99-101.

61 Recently: Boor, Myron and Bair, Jeffrey H., 'Suicide Rates, Handgun Control Laws, and Sociodemographic Variables', *Psychological Reports 66*, 1990: 923-30; Wasserman, Ira M., 'The Impact of Divorce on Suicide in the United States, 1970-1983', *Family Perspective 24*, 1990: 61-68; Stack, Steven, 'New Microlevel Data on the Impact of Divorce on Suicide, 1959-1980: A Test of Two Theories', *Journal of Marriage and the Family 52*, 1990: 119-27; Petronis, K.R., *et al*, 'An Epidemiologic Investigation of Potential Risk Factors for Suicide Attempts', *Social Psychiatry and Psychiatric Epidemiology 25*, 1990; Kowalski, Gregory S., 'Marital Dissolution and Suicide in the United States for the 1980s: A 10-Year Comparison', *Family Perspective 24*, 1990: 33-39; and Lester, David, 'A Regional Analysis of Suicide and Homocide Rates in the U.S.A.: Search for Broad Cultural Patterns', *Social Psychiatry and Psychiatric Epidemiology 23*, 1988: 202-05.

62 Stack, Steven, 'The Effect of Female Participation in the Labor Force on Suicide: A Time Series Analysis, 1948-1980', *Sociological Forum 2*, 1987: 257-74.

63 Stack, Steven, 'The Effect of Domestic/Religious Individualism on Suicide, 1954-1978', *Journal of Marriage and Family 45*, May 1985: 431-47.

64 Moens, Guido F.G., *et al*, 'Epidemiological Aspects of Suicide Among the Young in Selected European Countries', *Journal of Epidemiology and Community Health 42*, 1988: 279-85.

65 Warren, Lynda W. and Tomlinson-Keasey, C., 'The Context of Suicide', *American Journal of Orthopsychiatry 51*, January 1987, p. 42.

66 Stack, Steven, 'The Impact of Divorce on Suicide in Norway, 1951-1980' *Journal of Marriage and the Family 51*, 1989: 229-38.

67 Stack, Steven, 'The Effects of Suicide in Denmark, 1961-1980', *The Sociological Quarterly 31*, 1990: 361-68.

68 Kreitman, Norman and Casey, Patricia, 'Repetition of Parasuicide: An Epidemiological and Clinical Study', *British Journal of Psychiatry 153*, 1988: 792-800; Papathomopoulous, Evangelos, *et al*, 'Suicidal Attempts by Ingestion of Various Substances in 2,050 Children and Adolescents in Greece', *Canadian Journal of Psychiatry 34*, 1989: 205-09; Trovato, Frank and Vos, Rita, 'Domestic/Religious Individualism and Youth Suicide in Canada', *Family Perspective 24*, 1990; 69-81; Yang, Bijou U. and Lester, David, 'Fertility Rates and Suicide: Time Series Regional Studies', *Psychological Reports 64*, 1989: 676; and Asencio, A.P. *et al*, 'Epidemiology of Suicide in Valencia', *Social Psychiatry and Psychiatric Epidemiology 23*, 1988: 57-59.

69 Rosenfeld, Eva, 'Teenage Addiction', in *Problems of Addiction*, (ed), Bier, William C., New York: 1962.

70 Seldin, Nathan E., 'The Family of the Addict: A Review of the Literature', *The International Journal of the Addictions 7*, Spring 1972, 99, 106-17.

71 Chein, Isidor, Gerard, Donald L., Lee, Robert S. and Rosenfeld, Eva, *The Road To H: Narcotics, Delinquency, and Social Policy*, New York: Basic Books, 1964, pp. 253-57, 268-74, 312-19.

72 Noble, Peter, Hart, Tom and Nation, Ron, 'Correlates and Outcome of Illicit Drug Use by Adolescent Girls', *British Journal of Psychiatry 120*, 1972: 497-99.

73 Westby, William A. and Epstein, Nathan B., *The Silent Majority*, San Francisco: Jossey-Bass, 1969, pp. 4-6, 86, 102, 131, 156.

74 Blum, Richard H. *et al*, *Horatio Alger's Children*, San Francisco: Jossey-Bass, 1972, pp. 47-49, 58-61, 68-71, 85, 89, 91-92, 127-28, 274-75.

75 Kandel, Denise B., 'Drug and Drinking Behavior Among Youth', *Annual Review of Sociology 6*, 1980: 271.

76 Brook, Judith S., Whiteman, Martin and Scovell Gordon, Ann, 'Stages of Drug Use in Adolescence: Personality, Peer, and Family Correlates', *Developmental Psychology 19*, March 1983: 269-88.

77 Yamaguchi, Kazuo and Kandel, Denise B., 'On the Resolution of Role Incompatibility: A Life Event History Analysis of Family Roles and Marihuana Use', *American Journal of Sociology 90*, 1985: 1284-1325; and Yamaguchi and Kandel, 'Dynamic Relationships Between Premarital Cohabitation and Illicit Drug Use: An Event-History Analysis of Role Selection and Role Socialization', *American Sociological Review 50*, August 1985: 530-46.

78 Bowerman, C.E., and Elder Jr., G.H., 'Variations in Adolescent Perception of Family Power Structure', *American Sociological Review 29*, 1964: 551-67.

79 Marjoribanks, V., 'Environment, Social Class, and Mental Abilities', *Journal of Educational Psychology 63*, 1972: 103-07.

80 See: Tauber, M.A., 'Sex Differences in Parent-Child Interaction During a Free-Play Session', *Child Development 50*, 1979: 981-88; Macoby, E.E. and Jacklin, C.N. *The Psychology of Sex Differences*, Stanford: Stanford University Press, 1974; Lynn, D.B., *The Father: His Role in Child Development*, Monterey, CA: Brooks/Cole, 1974; Mutimer, Dorothy, *et al*, 'Some Differences in the Family Relationship of Achieving/Underachieving Readers', *The Journal of Genetic Psychology 109*, 1966: 67-74; Kimball, B., 'The Sentence Completion Technique in the Study of Scholastic Underachievement', *Journal of Consulting Psychology 16*, 1952: 353-58; Andersland, P.B., 'Parental Rejection and Adolescent Academic Achievement', *Dissertation Abstracts 28*, 1968: 11-B: 4751; Teahan, J.E., 'Parental Attitudes and College Success', *Journal of Educational Psychology 54*, 1963: 104-09; and Bing, Elizabeth, 'Effect of Childrearing Practices on Development of Differential Cognitive Abilities', *Child Development 34*, 1963: 631-48.

81 Robin, Monique, 'Neonate-Mother Interaction: Tactile Contacts in the Days Following Birth', *Early Child Development and Care 9*, 1982: 221-36; Robin, Monique and Josse, Denise, 'Maternal Language and the Development of Successive Infant Identities', *Early Child Development and Care 17*, 1984: 167-76; and Elbers, Locke, 'Sex Roles and Phonetic Factors in Parent Reference', *Journal of Child Language 13*, 1986: 429-30.

82 Sutton-Smith, B., *et al*,'Father-Absence Effects in Families of Different Sibling Compositions', *Child Development 39*, 1968: 1213-21; Douglas, J.W.B., *et al*, *All Our Future: A Longitudinal Study of Secondary Education*, London: Peter Davies, 1968, p. 188; Biller, Henry B., *Paternal Deprivation: Family, School, Sexuality, and Society*, Lexington MA: Lexington Books, 1974, p. 1131; Santrock, John W., 'Relation of Type and Onset of Father Absence to Cognitive Development', *Child Development 43*, 1972: 457-69; Zajone, R.B., 'Family Configuration and Intelligence', *Science 192*, 16 April 1976: 227-36; Shinn, Marybeth, 'Father Absence and Children's Cognitive Development', *Psychological Bulletin 85*, 1978: 295-324; Carlsmith, Lyn, 'Effect of early Father Absence on Scholastic Aptitude', *Harvard Educational Review 34*, 1964: 3-20.

83 Block, Jack, *et al*, 'Parental Functioning and the Home Environment in Families of Divorce: Prospective and Concurrent Analyses', *Journal of the American Academy of Child and Adolescent Psychiatry 27*, 1988: 207-13.

84 Bing, 'Effect of Childrearing Practices on Development of Differential Cognitive Abilities', pp. 64-65; Dyk, Ruth B.and Witkin, Hermann A., 'Family Experiences Related to the Development of Differentiation in Children', *Child Development 36*, 1965: 21-55; and Milner, Esther, 'A Study of the Relationship Between Reading Readiness in Grade One School Children and Patterns of Parent-Child Interaction', *Child Development 22*, 1951: 95-112.

85 Gold, D. and Andres, D., 'Developmental Comparisons Between 10-Year-Old Children with Employed and Non-employed Mothers', *Child Development 49*, 1978: 75-84. On the general literature, see: Montemayor, Rayond and Clayton, Mark D., 'Maternal Employment and Adolescent Development', *Theory into Practice 22*, 1983: 112-18.

86 Hill, Martha S. and Duncan, Greg T., 'Parental Family Income and the Socioeconomic Attainment of Children', *Social Science Research 16*, 1987: 39-73.

87 Stafford, Frank P., 'Women's Work, Sibling Competition, and Children's School Performance' *The American Economic Review 77*, 1987: 972-80.

88 Gil, David G., 'Violence Against Children', in *Child Abuse: A Reader and Source Book*, (ed) Leck, Constance M., 1978; reprint Open University Press, 1978, p. 49; Smith, Selwyn M., Hanson, Ruth and Noble, Sheila, 'Social Aspects of the Battered Baby Syndrome', in *Child Abuse: Commission and Omission*, (eds) Cook, Joanne V. and Bowles, Ray T., Toronto: Butterworths, 1980, pp. 217-20; Lightcap, Joy L., Kurland, Jeffrey A. and Burgess, Robert L., 'Child Abuse: A Test of Some Predictions form Evolutionary Theory', *Ethology and Sociobiology 3*, 1982: 64-65; Daly, Martin and Wilson, Margo, 'Child Abuse and Other Risks of Not Living with Both Parents', *Ethology and Sociobiology 6*, 1985: 197-209; and Sullivan, Richard, 'Admissions of Child Abuse Found to Drop Sharply', *New York Times*, 11 November 1985, p. A13.

89 A classic presentation of this argument is found in: Ross, Heather L. and Sawhill, Isabel V., *Time of Transition: The Growth of Families Headed By Women*, Washington DC: The Urban Institute, 1975, pp. 129-53.

90 White, James M., 'Premarital Cohabitation and Marital Stability in Canada', *Journal of Marriage and the Family 49*, 1987: 645-47; and Bumpass, Larry L. and Sweet, James A., 'National Estimates of Cohabitation: Cohort Levels and Union Stability', NSFH Working Paper No. 2, Centre for Demography and Ecology, University of Wisconsin at Madison, p. 10.

91 Booth, Alan and Johnson, David, 'Premarital Cohabitation and Marital Success', *Journal of Family Issues 9*, 1988: 261-70.

92 Yllo, Kersti and Straus, Murray A., 'Interpersonal Violence Among Married and Cohabitating Couples', *Family Relations 30*, 1981: 339-47.

93 Wiersma, Geertje Else, *Cohabitation, an Alternative to Marriage? A Cross-National Study*, Boston: Martinus Nijhoff, 1983, pp. 94-95.

From Household to Family to Individualism

Jon Davies

This essay deals with historical change in erotic and procreational behaviour—more usually, and perhaps more politely called 'family life'. Whatever it is called, it is essential to realise that while this essay does indeed have an historical orientation, i.e. it presents change as if one form of arrangement (in, say, the marriage ritual) is replaced by another, the 'replaced' ritual is not so much superseded as added to; and the history of such changes is more a process of uneven and selective incremental accretion rather than radically different stages: things change towards the future but not by jettisoning the past.

There is therefore no straightforward 'narrative' in this essay. The sub-title—From Household to Family to Individualism—does indeed imply an historical scheme; but embedded in it is a theme of continuity in the nature of the problems that were being addressed. This continuity or theme is that of the degree of internal and external stability in erotic and procreational arrangements, i.e. the nature of their articulation within the larger social system and the concomitant stabilities or instabilities that this articulation effected in the relationships between the adults and children involved in the business of adult sex, procreation and nurturance. Crucially, I am concerned with the stability or instability of intra-spousal and inter-generational relationships: and I hold the view that increasing and accelerating instability in intra-familial relationships is not a pathological deviation from an accidentally disturbed 'norm', but is a systemic part of our way of life ('late twentieth century capitalism' if you like), and a quite logical development from earlier arrangements. We are all individuals now.

64

Prologue

In the year 597 AD, the newly-arrived and rather anxious Augustine wrote from his fledgling 'diocese' in the pagan Kingdom of Kent to his sponsor, Pope Gregory the Great, to ask for guidance and advice on how properly to convert the 'barbarous, fierce and pagan nation' amongst which he found himself. Augustine was in large part seeking guidance on sexual matters: may a man, he asked, enter church after intercourse with his wife before he has washed himself? To what degree may the faithful marry with their kindred? May an expectant mother be baptised? May a man receive communion after he has had a sexually stimulating dream? 'The uncouth English', said Augustine, 'require guidance on all these matters.'[1]

Controlling the Brute Beast

The long-drawn out, and still continuing, process whereby Christian sexual ethics were constructed in and imposed upon Europe (and progressively upon other parts of the world) has never been anything other than a missionary effort; that is to say that their very formulation (never mind their promulgation) has always taken place in the face of more or less potent opposition from an endless series of 'uncouth' people—in Kent, Latin America, Africa... Whether because of recalcitrant human nature (Bede's 'barbarousness'), or because of ancient sexual codes ('paganism'), there has always been fierce resistance to some or all of the erotic and procreational theologies, ethical and philosophical systems of Christianity. The history of Christian sexual teaching, and the contemporary outcome of that history, can only be understood in the light of this essentially missionary experience with all that this means for the very precarious nature of the Christian accomplishment. All Christian proselytising in the area of sexual ethics has had to take very seriously indeed the power of the barbarous, fierce and pagan alternatives, not so much as competitors to be vanquished but as permanent, unvanquishable and barely containable rivals for the hearts, minds and genitals of adult men and adult women.

The word 'adult' is important. Christian teachers of sexual ethics assumed that they had before them the task of socialising and controlling adults, not (or not only) children; and that the task required endless reinforcement through an effective system of rewards, punishments and police power. Clerics knew only too well that the sexual rules and orders within their own ecclesiastical establishments were never sufficiently well internalised to be allowed to operate un-policed: and if this was true of clerics, then it was even more true of the laity, for 'If gold rusteth, what shall iron do?'.

Clearly there have been times when the Christian Establishment could feel itself to be and no doubt was very much more securely based than it was in those early days in Kent, whether because of a much firmer relationship with the secular authority (although the successor to Augustine's royal convert soon reverted to sexual paganism) or because of genuine popular support. By the Thirteenth Century, the English Church was both a central part of the nascent English State and a genuinely ubiquitous force and presence in the hamlets, villages and towns of the country. The parish system was by then pretty much in place, with a more or less integrated system of pastoral care and social control, mediated through priest, confessional and communicant congregation as well as through more formal judicial and semi-judicial courts, magistrates and lords of the manor.

There was, of course, a high degree of savagery in this social control system; women having babies outside marriage were routinely beaten 'until their bodies be bloodie'. Midwives were under instructions to withhold their ministrations to an unmarried woman in labour until her pain led her to confess the name of the man responsible; and women in general were kept in order by scares and accusations of witchcraft. The periodic witchcraft trials of some women kept all women under control and much of the content of witchcraft accusations was about sex. In *Malleus Maleficarum*, the Inquisitors handbook on the subject published in 1496, we read that a woman can be so 'darkened by the devil (that) she considers her husband so loathsome that not for all the world would she allow him to lie with her' (p. 139 of the 1986 edition, which reprints without comment the 1946 translator's description of the book as 'among the most important, wisest, and weightiest books in the world'!).[2] Not all of the victims were women: not all of the accusers were men.

We do not of course know how 'popular' this pastoral and parochial system was, either in the sense of being loved and valued, or in the sense of having successfully socialised at least the dominant section of the population into Christian values and associated behaviour. It would however be inconceivable that 600 years or so of systematic missionary activity, coupled with a 'punishment and reward' system affecting all areas of local and domestic life, could have failed to have at least got fixed firmly in people's minds the main features of Christian erotic and procreational teaching, if only as the major bulwark against ever-present temptation.

Marriage and Sex

In this developing ethic, erotic or romantic love was really rather a nuisance. There is no reason to assume that our forebears were indifferent to the happiness of their children but they realised (and we seem to have decided to forget) that happiness and sexual licence are not the same thing, and that the attractions of the flesh are no guarantor of marital stability. Where possible, and for the most sensible of reasons, attempts were made to explore compatibility (within a generally arranged system of marriage) by, for example, organising chaperoned experimental forms of courtship such as 'bundling', in which groups of (fully clothed) young people would be allowed to spend the night together to try to sort out some degree of mutual attraction.

In a hard world, however, it was clear that marriage needed a sombre and continuing form of social organisation and control. Love and respect were expected to *follow from* marriage rather than precede it, and this gradual process was also surrounded by a concerned but firm supervisory regimen. Romantic 'sex love' was regarded as a problem: European literature is full of minatory accounts of the personal tragedies and social uproars caused by giving in to the urgencies of the flesh. Lancelot and Guinevere followed Helen and Paris in destroying both themselves and the known civilised world and Romeo and Juliet troubled their kinfolk and came to a sad end.

Guided by the helpful repressions of the Catholic Church, our forefathers and foremothers lived under and within an explicit *system* of sexual ethics, ie. a more or less coherent system of prescriptions and proscriptions governing erotic and procreational life, a system structured by one ideal, that of total celibacy for everyone except (and even then only grudgingly) the duly married adult heterosexual procreational couple, for whom marriage was ordained *firstly* for the having and bringing up of children 'in the fear and nurture of the Lord.' This was not a system which respected the privacy of the marital bed. It was *an invasive system of sexual regulation* which sought to determine, for example, the frequency of sexual intercourse between husband and wife, the nature of the positions the married couple could adopt for sexual congress, the amatory use (if any) to be made of various parts of the body, and the amount of pleasure that the couple were entitled to feel as they pursued the procreational imperative upon each other's bodies.

Catholic theologians produced complex codes of sexual practice *for married people* (and for everyone else) which were then distributed as manuals—the Penitentials—to become part of the confessional and pastoral equipment of the parish priest. Peter Lombard held the essential Catholic view that it was a mortal sin to enjoy your wife merely to satisfy desire: sex between spouses was acceptable, i.e. was merely a venial sin, if it was engaged in for procreational purposes and in order to pay the 'conjugal debt'— that in order to support him or her in the struggle against temptation. (These two concerns lie behind the legitimation or non-criminalisation of marital rape, a legitimation only removed in 1991.) Sylvester (1515) was against non-coital sex (i.e. sex which did not lead to procreative sex) and against devices such as *coitus interruptus* but (in order to provide guidance for the anxious couple) he felt that an amatory process which *began* with the intention of consummating the act, but where for some reason later the man decided to stop, and did so with the consent of his wife, and withdrew but did not ejaculate—well, that was merely venial, and acceptable if:

> First, where they (non-coital sex) are not shameless touches proceeding from lust but from love, such as kisses and decent embraces. Second, where they in fact proceed from lust, but there is no thought of coition, so that it is neither intended nor excluded, and the place is suitable for

intercourse if the will for it ensues. Otherwise, they are mortal sins, because every lustful action that is not conjugal coitus or ordained to it actually or potentially is illicit.[3]

It is perhaps difficult to imagine how the average Catholic couple would make much sense of these rules; the effect of their existence would clearly surround the marriage bed with endless anxieties, as would the opinion in the *Malleus Maleficarum* that an unstirred male member was merely the sign of natural frigidity, but 'when it is stirred, and becomes erect, but yet cannot perform, it is a sign of witchcraft'.[4]

It is tempting to regard these 'manuals' with a degree of levity, as if they were the medieval equivalent of modern sex guides, with their performance-related indicators and anxious discussions about size, capacity and potency. Anxiety and confusions there must have been in the medieval bed—but fright and terror also, because these prescriptions were not just helpful guides to a better sex life, but invocations also of sanctions and punishment, and, to repeat, these were rules and controls of and on the sex life of married men and women. This was a system of control which had little time for what to us is the inviolable privacy of domestic life. Social control was exercised through the confessional and its associated system of penances, ostracisms and exclusions from communicant society, and by the rigorous punishment of sexual deviancy—deviancy, that is, from anything other than sanctioned, heterosexual (procreational) sex. The Church, that is the village Priest—the Father—supervised sexual life up to and into the marital bed, a bed to which the newly married couple would proceed at the end of the Nuptial Mass and to which they would be followed by the Priest—who would then sprinkle and bless both bed and dutifully bedded couple.

The medieval wedding service (one of the few bits of the liturgy written and used in the vernacular) required the new wife to be 'bonny and buxom in bed'—though the words do not quite mean what they may seem to us: they were more to do with obedience, in bed as elsewhere, than with advanced sexual technique. The 1662 version of the much older medieval service started off with a Homily which told the bride and groom that marriage:

is not by any to be enterprised, nor taken in hand, unadvisedly, lightly or wantonly, to satisfy men's carnal lusts and appetites, like brute beasts that have no understanding, but reverently, discreetly, advisedly, soberly, and in the fear of God: duly considering the causes for which matrimony was ordained.

First, It was ordained for the procreation of children, to be brought up in the fear and nurture of the Lord, and to the praise of his holy Name.

Secondly, it was ordained for a remedy against sin, and to avoid fornication; that such persons that have not the gift of continency might marry, and keep themselves undefiled members of Christ's body.

Thirdly, it was ordained for the mutual society, help and comfort, that the one ought to have of the other, both in prosperity and adversity...[5]

This service locates sex (ideally avoided completely, in keeping with the prior Christian value of celibacy) within the procreational and parenting duty: parents were responsible to God for their children. The Priest, armed with his Penitentials, and the local communicant society, armed with a very effective power of ostracism, provided an ever-present surveillance of the married life of the couple so consenting. There was no privacy: and while the sexual act itself was then as always an antic for two, marriage and procreation were matters of societal concern and regulation.

Household Formation

This ceaseless proselytising in the field of sexual ethics has its structural location in endlessly complex and frequently bitter negotiations between the interests of the kin and the interests of the Church. The Household or the Family developed out of this dialectic. The records we have are mostly those of the well-to-do; their property records (their wills for example) are more likely to have survived, but for the 'lower orders' as well, issues of property—field boundaries and hedges, ownership of tools or stands of timber, rights of access over fields, etc., were just as much caught up in communal and household life as they were for richer people. A peasant girl might bring little to the marriage in the way of capital beyond her own body and its fecundity, but they were crucial to the purpose of the marriage; and while not all dreams were realised, fewer nightmares would occur if husband and wife did indeed support each other and if their children did indeed honour them in their old age. The great and public wrangles between Church and kin, or later between Church and the State dynasty, may not have actually involved the lesser people directly, but they understood the importance of the issues because their own livelihoods depended on a successful solution of their own lesser versions of them.

It is clearly not the case that kin and Church clashed at every point. Land transfer systems dependent upon an exchange of virginal women (a very common form of kin-determined transaction) are clearly quite compatible with the Christian value of pre-marital chastity. Monogamy, and associated matters such as the degrees of affinity, cousin marriage and widow remarriage, and the legal status of concubines and bastards caused frequent disputes between Church and kin, and clerical attempts to control wills caused further trouble. Christian insistence on the voluntary nature of the marriage vows were clearly not compatible with whatever element of *coercion* there was in arranged, dynastic, marriages, but arranged marriage *per se* could easily be seen as quite compatible with the Church's concern for sobriety in the marital decision.

There were many points of straightforward conflict. An ecclesiastical vested interest in the propriety of individually alienable property—a propriety clearly the source of much of the land holding of the medieval Church—is not compatible with kin insistence on the collective ownership of such land and its concomitant inalienability by an individual, no matter how senior that individual might be. There would be serious arguments at times of, say, a conversion of the senior male of the household, when this conversion was accompanied by the gifting of land or revenue to the Church. The same would apply when a will provided for the financing of a chantry out of an estate which the kinfolk regarded as 'theirs'.

Even here, however, the interests of kin and Church could coincide. The conveyance of land, or the rents from land, from kin to a local monastery or convent was one way of actually keeping it in the family when the abbot or abbess was a celibate younger brother or sister with no immediate family to support or satisfy. Such arrangements were particularly valuable for a military ruling class, for example at Crusading times, when for the departing and perhaps never-to-return warrior, the Church was the best bank and deed-depository precisely because it was run by relatives—or at least by relatives who (because they were celibate) were to some extent located outside the only too common intra-kin disputes about ownership and control.

The popularity of the Church did not, of course, increase when it got involved in such intra-kin quarrels—especially if the outcome was the transfer to the Church of the property under dispute.

Conflicts between Church and kin, or between the sexual ethics and self-interest of the Church and the dynastic ambitions of dominant and predatory men were endemic in medieval society, moderated perhaps because both the sexual ethics of the Church and the pecuniary interests of both kin and Church came together in insisting that the marrying business was sensibly and primarily the concern of 'third parties' (themselves) and only secondarily the concern of the 'loving' couple itself. At every level of society, 'coupling' becomes marriage by being written into the broader practical considerations of household, kin and community; it involved entering a status fixed into the structures and concerns of others, and not a means of satisfying oneself.

Needless to say, men controlled the business at all points and at all levels of society. The 'kin' who arranged the marriages were the senior men; the 'Church' was men. Women were not the only ones whose wishes were ignored or over-ridden: young men too (including young royal men) could find themselves persuaded, cajoled or coerced into tactical rather than romantic marriages. But the same young men would at some time find themselves succeeding to the controlling role, whereas women rarely would. Women might indeed have power behind the scenes—but the scenes themselves were set by men.

Over the centuries, Christian sexual ethics, and in particular the sets of rules to do with marriage, represent a compromise between the interests of the kin and the teaching and ambitions of the Church. In simple terms, the kin was allowed to arrange the marriage, ie. to sort out the contractual business of betrothal; the church insisted on sanctifying the actual marriage on the implicit premise of it being a ceremony entered into by voluntary agreement between two adults. A sanctified contract satisfied both parties.

Over hundreds of years, and with endless permutations at times of political change, war, economic growth and urbanisation etc., etc., this is what marriage was for our ancestors: a matter sensibly and formally organised by the kin, but sanctioned and sanctified by the church (and therefore the state) and as such, an eminently socially located act, providing (or oppressing!) the participants with a range of connected relatives and interested parties who could be counted upon to help out (stick their noses in) when as and while the marriage found itself in difficulties. Sex was regulated inside and outside marriage. Celibacy was the ideal: and chastity the operative norm: divorce did not exist.

This process of carefully surrounding young people with adult support started early on with the institution of god-parents and continued to protect both young and old in various forms of semi-contractual arrangements covering such things as widowhood or 'retirement'. An old farmer would agree to vacate the farmhouse and land, and hand it on to his eldest son (who was then and therefore able to marry) as long as the son would contract to provide the old man and his wife with food, fuel and lodging for as long as they lived. In such a system it was possible to divorce neither one's spouse, nor one's parents, nor children, nor aunties, nor cousins; and household life was lived within a hierarchy of rationed ambition.

From Household to Family

Wherever we are now, we are not there. Analyses and descriptions of how we moved from there to here vary enormously in their emphases. Marxists stress the power of material factors and locate sexual change within alterations in the labour market and in the related changes in the means of production. Theologians focus on the primacy of events such as the Reformation and Counter Reformation. Protestants saw and see in the end of a repressive and invasive system of sexual regulation an enhancing of the autonomy of 'the family' exalting, as Steven Ozment puts it,

> the patriarchal nuclear family as the liberation of men, women and children from religious, sexual and vocational bondage.[6]

A Catholic view of these events will see the disruption of the religious monopoly and authority of the medieval Church by Protestant Reformers as leading gradually but inevitably to excesses of uncontrolled and therefore uncontrollable individualism and hedonism, in particular in sexual matters, and Ozment's own title indicates that whatever 'liberation' there might have been was not experienced equally by all parties concerned in the centuries that followed the Reformation.

Psychoanalysts have their own view of history, seeing it as some kind of hydraulic system in which what is repressed at one time will inevitably pop up sometime else, all the stronger for being repressed, and determined to impose the repressions of licence upon the repressions of authority. Anthropologists and sociologists give us fairly clear pictures of the family evolving out of the household and away from effective kin-based systems; and historians and literary commentators trace the same evolution in the relations between the sexes, in parental practice and in the whole elaboration of a way of life in which 'affect' (affection?) is increasingly the exclusive concern of the family whose members otherwise find themselves in an impersonal and indifferent world. To indicate the range of argument on these points, Marxists for example totally refute the last, rather important school of thought, insisting that there can be no haven against the on-rush of capitalism: 'The bourgeoisie has torn away from the family its sentimental veil, and has reduced the family relation to a mere money relation.'[7]

The catch-phrase which perhaps best summarises these changes is '**Liberty Equality Fraternity**'. Liberty and Equality have probably been the ones which have been most overworked; and—in particular for discussions of the changes in domestic affairs over the last four hundred years—it perhaps makes some sense to look at the very much less used concept, that of **Fraternity**, if only because embedded in it is what is perhaps the major contemporary problem for libertarian individualistic doctrines, viz. the issue of female 'emancipation'. In a Europe no longer under one religious and ethical system, European sailors, merchants and soldiers began to set off on those astonishing journeys which over several centuries created a 'world economy', involving huge movements of populations in which family life would be subjected to the 'strains of the great migrations, wars and dispersals' which Michael Novak sees as being paralleled in contemporary times by other forms of strain arising out of the great mobility encouraged by and in free societies.[8] In this great mobility—'not only geographic but in regions of the heart'[9] lay both the promise and the problem of family life in the West.

Fraternity

The Reformation and the turmoil which preceded and followed it both built upon and changed the medieval system, with the full effect of these changes being of course exported across the Atlantic to the American colonies—and re-exported centuries later. In England, in a structural sense, the Reformation's attack on Church property reshuffled the property settlements of centuries, liquidated some of the accumulated assets of the Church and fed land and wealth back into the ceaseless dynastic struggles of the landed gentry (some up, some down).

There had long been an active land market in England, and the sale of Church lands gave this market a major boost—rather like the 'privatisation' schemes of the last ten years. The Crown increasingly replaced the Church as the legal arbiter of property matters; and English national politics then became in large measure an attempt to divorce the Crown from the State in order to be able to endow the institutions of the State with at least the semblance of impartiality—or, failing that, to make them 'representative' of, that is to say exploitable by, the landed classes. The power of aristocratic kin was re-asserted through various forms of cheerful predatory nepotism, regarded as a perfectly legitimate private utilisation of the 'places' of public life.

The Reformation had however provided an effective ideology for a form of family life other than the reinvigorated traditional nepotism of the aristocracy. A shift in moral power followed the destruction of the universal Church. A world of religious pluralism necessarily gave rise to demands for 'freedom of conscience', that is to say for the drawing of a line between the public and the private: indeed, the very concept of 'the private' enters the debate. Once admitted, this is a concept of substantial elasticity; and freedom of conscience and an insistence on privacy in the religious sphere quite readily translated into demands for freedom of conscience and privacy in the household or family.

Freedom of conscience did not, of course, mean freedom from conscience. The teaching and inculcation of morality had to be located somewhere: and after some serious attempts at theocracy, the Protestant Reformers transformed the agency of universal repression from an external church (which like all external authorities could from time to time be avoided or at least sniggered at) into the unavoidable, internalised, self-imposed Voice of Conscience, which never sleeps, not even when we do. The inner Voice of Conscience replaced the external Voice of Authority—and probably had to, because the Reformation and the ensuing struggles had destroyed for ever the timeless, unitary authority of the Catholic Church.

The only possible location, in a pluralist society, of a mechanism for internalising such a variety of forms of conscience was parental power, exercised within a nuclear family, itself heavily bounded over and against the outside world. Only in such an institution, in which parents (ie. the father) combined the powers of church and state, could effective socialisation of the new breeds of youngsters take place—and for a new purpose; ie. the pursuit of individual betterment, in which the success of the new generation was to lie precisely in the extent to which it jettisoned rather than repeated the lessons and examples of the older generation. Medieval parents were punished if they educated their children to a station or ambition above their own; bourgeois parents are punished (by conscience) if they fail to do precisely that. (They are punished by success when they succeed.) The substantive moral or sexual regimen stayed pretty much the same—a repressive channelling of eroticism into procreational dutiful sex. The Church Father was replaced by The Father—the *pater familias*, now appearing as undisputed Head of the Family.

With the failure of the Protestant attempt to establish a theocracy, Privacy—the freedom to do what one liked within the boundary of one's home—becomes the insistent value. After some resistance (and persecution) domestic privacy becomes accepted as the best (or least worst) agency of general socialisation within a pluralist culture: 'The Family' is now expected to do on its own what Church and State and Kin had previously done together. Bunyan stated that 'The fruits of true Christianity flow from a proper fulfilment of duties between husband and wife, parents and children', while Calvin was (as usual) even more insistent: 'Those who violate the parental authority by contempt or rebellion are not men but monsters. Therefore the Lord commands all those who disobey their parents are to be put to death'.[10]

Amongst the slowly developing middle classes, and the respectable lower classes from which they came, the boundary between the public and the private is just as adamantly maintained against the claims of an endless array of kinfolk as against the truculent pretensions of the Crown (State) and the admonitory injunctions of the Priest (Church). **Fraternity** which states that 'All men are my brothers' means that 'No man is my Brother'. It also means that no man is my Keeper—which of course means that I cannot be expected to look after/be responsible for anyone else—or that I can expect to be able to call on anyone else to be responsible for me. The Family, cut off from the oppressively supportive kin and communal network, is an inherently unstable device: and it is meant to be.

This is a point that bears stressing. Fraternity, that is to say the freedoms that men sought to establish between themselves, was not simply freedom in the political sphere: it entailed freedom from obligations to kin as well as from the injunctions of the Church and the pretensions of the Crown. The word 'Fraternity' spelt the end of the acceptance of the web of kinship loyalties and obligations which so slow down the efforts of the determined individualist; or, to put it another way, Fraternity removed the disincentive effect of having too many people to fall back on. Fraternity is the opposite of nepotism, a system which lay at the heart of medieval and early modern dynastic life. Fraternity is the language of individualism, a doctrine hostile to the pretensions of a patriarchical Monarch, to the authority of the Reverend Father—and to the traditional claims of one's relatives. All men are equal because they are all equally brothers; sibling hierarchy disappears along with all other notions of ascriptive status (we are talking initially about theory here), and the universal fraternity of all becomes the particular Brotherhood of None.

Fraternity did not, however, mean a re-ordering of life for women. There was to be neither extra equality nor extra liberty for women; nor sorority, since women, always defined by their relationship to men, were now exclusively and adamantly defined by their relationship to the man to whom they were married: their blood relatives gave them away. In the great moral tract of English Protestantism, Pilgrim's Progress, it is the man on his own who undertakes and makes the Journey:

> The man [Christian] began to run. Now, he had not run far from his own door but his wife and children [perceiving it] began to cry after him to return; but the man put his fingers in his ears, and ran on, crying Life! Life! Eternal Life! So he looked not behind him, but fled towards the middle of the plain [toward the shining light].[11]

Before his running off, Christian had found that his wife and children had been rather insensitive to his troubles: they had exhibited a 'harsh and surly carriage' towards him. However, at the end, mission accomplished, Christian sends for his wife and children, whose access to the Gate of Heaven is essentially assured by his, Christian's, success and not by their own merit or virtue.

In the great moral tract of English political economy, Robinson Crusoe, women do not appear at all. (The Swiss Family Robinson, another island story, has women—and therefore sex—in it and they cause a deal of trouble—but then foreigners are like that.) In 1867 Offenbach turned Robinson Crusoe into an operetta in which Man Friday becomes a woman and in which Crusoe has a wife back home in Bristol. Years before, in the sequel to Robinson Crusoe, Defoe describes how his returned hero is prevented from going on further voyages because of his pregnant wife. She however is aware that she is 'an obstruction', and she dies in childbirth—and Crusoe sails away, leaving his children behind.[12] Gulliver, on his return from an idyllic sojourn amongst the Houyhnhnm, and after many years absence from wife and children, is filled with 'Hatred, Disgust and Contempt' at the sight of them, and faints when his wife ('that odious Animal') kisses him.[13] The Travelling Man gets to see the world: his lonely journeys create in him the necessary dissatisfactions of ambition: the woman waits—for happy reunion or rejection.

The Protestant Family

The Protestant Family becomes the private sphere, the location of individualism. The 'individualism' this moral world celebrated is an individualism of men, with women-and-children simply annexed as one dependent part of Man. Bunyan's metaphysic has two kinds of human beings in it: (1) Pilgrim-Men; and (2) Women-and-children. Men are mobile; women wait. Christian, Crusoe and Gulliver can become individuals, or become who they are, only via tension with their families—with fathers in the case of sons, with wives in the case of husbands.

Fissionable relationships make up the central moral drama of these families. Robinson Crusoe is the story of a man who has a quarrel with his father and who therefore runs away to sea. It is a kind of anglicised Oedipus story, with the sex taken out: not only does it start with a Father-Son conflict, but it continues with a rather corrosive view of the relationships between the generations: Robinson's inheritance ('cascading down the generations') is a wreck! It is, however, a useful wreck—made useful, of course, by Robinson's work. Robinson's quarrel with his father and the concomitant vacating of the family home is precisely what makes a man of him, and which at the end of the book enables him to return home to be reconciled with his (now-dead) father, on the basis of an achieved equality/fraternity. Freud will later rediscover the origins of individualism in that structured instability of intra-generational relations within the nuclear family which he called the Oedipus complex.

The stories of both Bunyan and Defoe are stories of Journeys. Men—again and again, *Men*—must leave the family home in order to find salvation in order to better themselves. Journeys can be either social journeys (what sociologists call social mobility) or geographical journeys or, as in the case of many a Dick Whittington, both. The pre-Reformation moral system was offended by too much 'journeying' because it depended more upon effective policing than upon internalised belief for the maintenance of social order; and policing could only be effective in a pre-literate culture when the population was immobile and therefore familiar. The laws of settlement and acts against vagrancy sought to enforce a moral order via a system of face to face familiarity between the policers and the policed. As social and geographical mobility increased, and came to be seen as both legitimate and beneficial, then social order could better be ensured via an enhanced system of early and effective socialisation *of children*, under and in which the necessary social values could be deeply internalised—and therefore capable of stand-alone operation, no longer requiring ubiquitous policing. Internalised values are travelling values. Successful parents are precisely those made redundant by the higher accomplishments and mobility of their children: Christian's parents are not mentioned at all and Crusoe's helpfully oppressive father is dead by the time he returns home—having performed the necessary task of driving the young man away in a suitably rebellious state of mind.

For the male, the patriarchal nuclear family was, of all domestic arrangements, most likely to be compatible with individualism *and* mobility, with security in early childhood and instability in early adulthood—Crusoes Pere et Fils. In particular, boys become men by excelling over their fathers. Girls, on the other hand, become women by emulating their mothers. In such a society, childhood socialisation is primarily a matter of internalising (and for boys transcending) the adult, parental example: it depends upon the singularity, idiosyncrasy even, of parental practice. All parents are incompetent. They may have either read about or been given instruction in the business of becoming *a* parent—but no system of prior instruction can ever prepare, say, the girl who becomes the wife of *this* husband for what happens when she also becomes the mother of *this* child and he becomes the father of *this* child and the husband of *this* mother, who is now no longer simply *a* wife but *this/his* wife.....

The Pre-Reformation system had understood this: and had provided, or imposed a regulatory system of parental supervision, ie. a system which supervised *adult* parents and their children, and did this in a rural culture which was resistant to change or which at least insisted on managing change through the exercise of proper authority. An 'Open Society' emerging out of this culture, and seeing its prosperity as dependent upon innovation and expansion, and seeing these as in turn dependent upon self-seeking individualism, would (amongst other things) feel its way towards a form of family structure which would maximise idiosyncrasy and minimise inter-generational dependency.

The emerging middle-class nuclear family did precisely this: it was and is a self-liquidating institution, organised for its own end. This was a major departure and indeed at its birth and throughout its existence the nuclear family has been under attack by the more radical traditionalisms of (1) aristocratic practices, which retain dynastic concerns for permanency: (2) romanticisms of one type or another, which in true medieval style pine for an equation of love with tragedy and (3) sundry collectivisms, nostalgic for release from the burden of individualism. In order in part to cope with the virulence of these oppositions, the nascent bourgeois nuclear family rooted itself initially in the most long-lived of all traditions—male supremacy: this has continued through all known forms of domesticity: Men, in society or at home, are a caste—*the* caste. Fraternal society is a society of men: the exemplary figures of such a society are the lonely examples of Christian and Crusoe. Women are located in eager passivity, brought back to life by the return of the active individual man.

The 'Individualism' of Bunyan and Defoe is an individualism centred on an image of a Man and his dependants—which he may, as in the case of Christian, simply abandon. Whether the Man stays attached or not, his identity is held to contain the identities of his wife and children. F.A. Hayek, for example, is very explicit:

> in the language of the great writers of the eighteenth century, it was man's 'self-love', or even his 'selfish interests', which they represented as the 'universal mover'... These terms, however, did not mean egotism in the narrow sense of concern only with the immediate needs of one's proper person. The 'self', for which alone people were supposed to care, did as a matter of course include their family and friends.[14]

This was not a 'typically male' oversight by Hayek: he based the entire validity of his individualism on membership of such voluntary groups—of which the family, he very mistakenly implies, was one. Adam Smith certainly seems to have seen women fairly firmly located at home: his strictures on the 'Institutions for the

Education of Youth' are clearly about male youth only, for he contrasts such institutions with 'public institutions for the education of women' which, he notes with approval, did not exist:

> There are no public institutions for the education of women, and there is accordingly nothing useless, absurd or fantastical in the common course of their education. They are taught what their parents and guardians judge it necessary or useful for them to learn; and they are taught nothing else. Every part of their education tends evidently to some useful purpose; either to improve the natural attractions of their person, or to form their mind to reserve, to modesty, to chastity, and to oeconomy; to render them both likely to become the mistress of a family and to behave properly when they become such. In every part of her life a woman feels some conveniency or advantage from every part of her education.[15]

Eleanor Rathbone discusses Smith's view of the relationship between the manual workers wages and 'his' being responsible for bringing up a family[16] and Michael Novak continues this tradition, ie. of an individualism rooted in a rather unquestioned institution. In *The Spirit of Democratic Capitalism* we read that 'The self is primarily familial'; and that 'in the moral order the primary institution of realism is the bourgeois family'. However, he also states that 'For generations, political theory, economic theory, and moral theory—pre-occupied with the individual and the state—have systematically neglected the social vitality of the family.'[17] It is now necessary to have look at the kind of 'family' which is now succeeding the 'bourgeois family' which emerged into and out of the eras of Fraternity.

Families For Capitalism: from status to contract.

In *The Explanation of Ideology*, Immanuel Todd argues that there is a clear relationship between family type and societal organisation: and that the causal relationship goes from the former to the latter: 'family relations between parents and children, between husband and wife, provide a model for political systems and serve to define the relationship between the individual and authority.[18] For our purposes, he can be taken to mean that the capitalist-democratic West is the result of a family style which maximises fissionable relationships between the generations—crucially, between fathers and sons: in what Todd calls the 'absolute nuclear family' the possibility of disinheritance combined with the right of the generations to have nothing whatsoever to do with each other produce a system of maximum freedom (or maximum insecurity), ie. of maximum individuation.

This freedom, to repeat a point made earlier, is a freedom both of one generation from another and the freedom of the members of one generation from one another. Brothers are no more obliged to be engaged in business, or to even associate with brothers than are fathers with sons; and where such relationships may indeed exist they will be grounded in contracts contrived for mutual benefit rather than in the unvarying inexplicit prescriptions of tradition. These are the family styles of men on the make in and for a society which, unceasingly, requires making and remaking.

In empirical terms, such family styles are to be found, as Todd shows, in the Anglo-Saxon West, where the pursuit of wealth, career and A-levels creates a steady flow of self-improving people, in which the latest generation will feel it has failed if it does no better than its progenitor and where siblings are not expected to be any more economically co-operative with each other than with complete strangers. In economic terms, this produces an open society, a society in which the individual energies released by this radical discarding of inter and intra-generational obligations produces both hard work and open-mindedness—hard work rewarded by hard cash and open-mindedness rewarded by political freedom and creativity, deeply hostile to dogma and dogmatic authority.

The basic value system which makes such a society possible is a generalised value which denies primacy to any particular substantive moral system. Tolerance and pluralism, within the broadest possible limits, are what makes this society possible. This includes the structured possibility of getting things wrong. This is in no way to imply that this is a society without morals: but it is a society with a variety of attitudes, of which the most basic is the inadvisability of dogma. In theological terms, it is the openness of *The Courage to Be*[19] and not the closed-ness of *The Imitation of Christ*[20] that is most appropriate. Crudely, when failure has a systemic function, there is no overriding reason to know where you are going until you've actually been there—and if you are wrong, then someone else, though not everyone else, benefits.

For Talcott Parsons,[21] as for most writers on the family, values are more experienced as examples and as embodiments than learnt from formal presentations; values walk around the house, they are the presence of a Mother or the (equally significant) absence of a Father. Freud (often complimented by the criticism that all he understood was the bourgeois nuclear family) provided an analysis and an imagery for the internal relations of a family life located within this open society: the Oedipal conflict denotes the positive functions of inter-generational tension, which has the effect of ensuring the venturing into the world, under conditions of considerable insecurity, of one of the sons at least. It also, of course, has the effect of impressing upon the father the fact that he should in no way rely on his sons: as Talcott Parsons points out, family life has, over and above the function of socialising the young, the function of stabilising the adult personalities of the parents, and this stabilisation takes place as much in inter-generational as in inter-spousal transactions and tensions.

Inevitably, it is the sexual, and specifically the sexually repressive aspect of Freud's writing that has received most attention —and caused most derision. No doubt, as increasing numbers of men and women saw in capitalism a chance (for once and for all?) to take themselves and their progeny out of the huge collective repression of poverty, then they were indeed likely to assume that a small amount of sexual repression at home was worth a large amount of liberty and material well-being abroad: and Freud's writing can be read as a commentary on the good sense of the sexual economy of a gradually more confident upwardly mobile middle class—of which there had always been singular examples, but which were now becoming quite normal. Marx and Engels, displaying in this area of social analysis (at least) a cheerful disregard for facts, chose to regard these 'bourgeois' families as rooted in nothing other than repression and exploitation. The great Marxist tract on the family (the *Origin of the Family Private Property and the State*) claims that only amongst the proletariat are the relationships between men and women founded on mutual respect and affection, while in the bourgeois family, where marriages (claims Engels) are rooted in materialism, married life is loveless and characterised by faithlessness (by both sexes) and squalid sex. In fact, as Peter Gay shows in his important book *Education of the Senses*,[22] family life amongst the growing numbers of middle class families was steadily reaping the benefit of its own success.

The gradual provision of genuinely 'private' houses transformed the opportunities for intimacy, self-expression and mutual sexual discoveries. In 1851, in the central areas of Newcastle upon Tyne, 60 per cent of families lived in one room in a rookery occupied by large numbers of families similarly accommodated. Such a style of life has now disappeared. 'Our own front door' and 'indoor toilets' and 'master bedrooms' indicated privacy not only of the family over and against all other families, but of some parts and some activities of the family over and against other parts and activities of the family. As Peter Gay shows, this enhanced privacy—the steady advance of bourgeois culture—created opportunities for home-based transactions and intimacies of a cheerfully unrepressed but privately expressed nature.

Middle class families were the first to adopt contraception (and the most vociferous in denying it), thereby beginning the separation of sex-as-pleasure from sex-for-conception; and it is hard to believe that they did this because some version of the Welfare State was there to handle whatever mistakes might occur. Over the late nineteenth and early twentieth century, what were once the fairy-tale romances exclusive to Prince and Princess became the ordinary experience and expectation of many ordinary respectable people: capitalism had succeeded—it provided what was wanted as a reward for what had been achieved. Who needed the Pumpkin and the Palace when you had the car and 34 Laburnum Drive?

The recently published *Forever England: Femininity, Literature and Conservatism Between the Wars*[23] complements Peter Gay's work, in showing how domesticated romance became, for many people, a generally civilised way of having children, avoiding loneliness and of finding meaning in life. Western economies grew on the back of great and small journeys—of Columbus to American and Cook to Australia, of Welsh miners to Pennsylvania, of Scottish peasants to New Zealand; and, perhaps just as importantly, though less dramatically, of many millions of men to work in the morning, away from home, but returning every evening to an establishment increasingly containing within its walls the material and emotional and carnal delights hitherto found only in music halls, fairy-tales and dreams: the average semi detached house had within it more affluent contrivances and capital goods than most of the magnificent palaces of the past. Gradually, the home became the object and expression, for both men and women, of consumer capitalism.

In *Family Socialisation and Interaction Process*, Talcott Parsons[24] shows that by this century the nuclear family was the dominant form of household in the capitalist West. Our fathers grew up in two generational co-habiting private families, which were created by a formalised and voluntary union of two heterosexual adults, whose romantic love was turned into the basis of parenthood in which one adult (Mother) took on, as a permanent and full time occupation, the business of child care and in which the other adult (Father) took on the equally permanent and full-time responsibility for earning a living for the family. Parenthood was synonymous with adulthood—or vice versa. Love was spousal and parental love: in the words of the song 'They were so in love for the family.'

Parental love was almost totally altruistic. Parents did not expect their children to be financially responsible for them in their old age, still less to actually repay them, in material kind, for the large amounts of money conferred upon children and young people over the course of their lengthy dependency. Equally, those dependency periods are very definitely expected to come to a clear and definite end. While private and public pension schemes (one of the great inventions of capitalism) have replaced the financial responsibility of the young for the old, the young, once independent, are in turn meant to stay that way. This is symbolised by the fact that our society ('the West') is unique in conferring upon the older generation the legal option of disinheriting the young. The young, however, will, when they depart, leave a stable unit: their going is within, not against, the nature of things: nuclear families exist in order to bring about their own end—in good time (one of Oedipus's offences was to get the timing wrong). For perhaps the first half of this century the family form and sexual regimen for which our forebears in the nineteenth century were struggling seems to have been reasonably well established. Geoffrey Gorer[25] and Steve

Humphries[26] both document the successful accomplishment of a repressive, family-based erotic and procreational life.

This seems to have changed rather quickly. In 1973 Michael Young and Peter Willmott wrote *The Symmetrical Family*. This strangely sanguine book saw the family not as the main 'haven in a heartless world' but as a social construction characterised by calculated mutuality and conjugality. It combines, they said, 'altruism with self-interest' and this has made it more united. The idea of symmetry—ie. in which there are no exclusive roles for men or for women—would remove inter-gender friction, because 'women would have as much right as men to seek, and to gain, fulfilment out of the home as in it'. Feminism, the authors felt, would lead to greater symmetry in that both men and women would be doing two demanding jobs apiece (two inside the home and two outside) and while this might very well lead to more

> family failures..(this) is not necessarily disastrous. The people we inter-viewed who had married more than once did not appear any less content than others. But we did not see the children, and it is they and the divorced spouses who do not remarry who are commonly the victim. The family may well 'cease to be a haven for children', but the adults concerned, 'once they have had a brief encounter with their biological urges' will find fulfilment in jobs inside and outside the home. Will this mean that such a family will 'have very little for its members to live for beyond themselves? Itself fostering a general social isolation-ism? Perhaps so...'[27]

(The rather insouciant 'perhaps so' seems to stem from the author's concluding view that the affluence which had brought about 'symmetry' was about to give way to serious ecological and economic problems which would somehow create an ascetic egalitarianism in which everyone would help every one else rather than rely (be forced to rely) on the members of this kind of 'family'.)

There is to be found in this quotation the contemporary solution to the problems which were built into the domestic structures of Fraternity. The erotic basis of marriage (to repeat, of marriage) which so concerned or obsessed our medieval forebears is now reduced to an impersonal itch (biological urges of a brief encounter kind), while the procreative side of marriage, ie. children, are hardly considered at all. Sex is seen as something which adults contract to do between, with and for themselves, for as long as it suits them and not (as the quotation makes clear) an activity which, as intimacy and procreation, elaborates or is grounded in or gives rise to an identity, a status, a permanency.

Young's is the language of *contract*, a relationship valid for adults only. The contract—the marriage, or the 'relationship'—lasts only for so long as the 'symmetry', the mutual benefit, persists: these are contracts rooted in anticipated cessation, with an 'at arms length' caveat on every page. Thus for example Ms Tibe Aleksander says in *The Independent* on 1 March 1992 'the harsh reality is that many co-habitation relationships don't last for ever. Unless you consider your legal and financial position at the start you could end up losing everything.' (Strange indeed is a world in which the upholders of traditional marriage rather than such 'relationships' are held to be unromantic!).

Behind these formulations of the late twentieth century there are several decades of egalitarian or libertarian attempts to replace the domestic fixed-status structures of Fraternity with the open society of contract. Starting perhaps with the first successful divorce case brought by a woman (1801), and running through the issue of married women's property, to the suffrage argument, the matter of married women's competence to engage independently in contracts or give independent evidence in court or to determine abortion decisions or to control her sexual availability within the marriage, or to retain occupation and ownership of domestic property and to determine, via custody orders, the upbringing of the family progeny, etc, etc—all of these changes have been rooted in the idea of contract. From that premise there can be little legitimation of coerced or unequal relations between adult men and women, any more than between adult men. Indeed, inasmuch as sex is simply for sex only (whatever that means), then the notion of contract flows along very easily indeed with the freedom from control of all sexual relations between consenting (contracting) adults. So Hayek, for example, can quote with evident approval Bertrand Russell's 1955 article in favour of equal legal treatment of homosexual practices, and comments that 'Private practice among adults, however abhorrent it may be to the majority, is not a proper subject for coercive action for a state whose object is to minimise coercion.'[28]

Sex, then, is 'an urge', an inherently impersonal and private thing, a matter of convenience (or inconvenience), a *contra*-ception. Marriage, if it has much point at all, is a temporary incarnation of that urge; and as a contract it is merely one form of many within which adult men and women can, whether with other adult men or adult women, and whether for five minutes or five years, attend to their urges. There is no sexual ethic, no sexual system, no evaluation of sexual acts in terms of extrinsic purpose (eg. GOD), and therefore, given the contractual basis of these various transactions, and given adult participants, there is no call to surround sexual activity with any rules other than the ordinary day to day rules of advertising and caveat emptor, such as appear for example in the Sausage Rolls and Meat Pie Regulations (1976) or 'Health' warnings on cigarette packets. To slightly adapt the Communist Manifesto: these changes have stripped away from the family its sentimental veil and reduced the family relation to a mere genital relation. In a strange way, this idea of sex and marriage is the same as that medieval view which also regarded marital (procreative) sex as incompatible with romantic, lustful, sex. The difference is, of course, that the Church for that reason preached the avoidance of lust, whereas the modern view preaches its pursuit.

Children—Free At Last

What, though, about the children—those human beings to whom Michael Young did not even speak? The Church of England Alternative Service Book (1980), apart from enriching the English language and the Anglican liturgy, reversed two millennia of religious teaching when it demoted children from their first place in the priorities of marriage—it replaces them with the adults. *If the point and purpose of marriage is located in a contract between adults, then by definition children, qua children, can not be parties to the marriage.*

For children there are therefore only two options: either family life must be regarded as merely another voluntary institution, in which the rather inescapable fact of their involuntary membership of it must be compensated for by maximising their freedom within and from it—including, obviously, the freedom to leave it; and, the second and complementary option, children must be seen as not really 'belonging' to these specific parents but as the responsibility of society at large. Given that, then the actual status of a child as the child of particular parents ('legitimate' or 'illegitimate') becomes irrelevant—as the Conservative Government recognised when in the 1980s it went through all legislation and related documents removing the word 'illegitimate', just as the Labour Party once did when it removed from the statutes all references to 'The Working Classes'.

It is of course easier to alter the law than biology: and sexual freedom for children can only too easily result in female children becoming very young and very isolated mothers. Julie, a pregnant 15 year old, and one among 120,000 teenage pregnancies in 1991 (England and Wales) knew that her behaviour had upset her family. She told the *Newcastle Journal* on 30 December 1991 that her grandmother had 'said that I had disgraced the family, but I think she has forgiven me now... My 16 year old boyfriend's parents have only just started talking to me again, they said I had ruined their son's life.' Julie was very much in need of 'community support' as was, in a different context, 'mother-of-two and divorcee Barbara Gubbins', media manager with Albion Graphics and Marketing, who wanted to work and who also wanted 'the community' to accept an obligation for rearing her (and her divorced husband's) children): she wanted

> Tax concessions related to child care payments, tighter maintenance controls, extra child allowance, seasonal holiday grants, swap shops and after-school twilight activities, further creche and day care facilities for children. In order for a woman to work, she has to have a reasonably good salary to meet the child care rates, a reasonable employer to allow her flexibility to attend essential events and a reasonably fit family to assist with illness and holiday cover.[29]

When marriage is seen as a contract—or, more accurately, when marriage is seen as a contractual 'relationship', then not only does it becomes the job of 'society' or the state to step in to identify and defend the interests of those who, though non-participant to the contract, are (out of no choice of their own) both involved and affected, (the baby and children in the two cases above), but it also has to step in to defend the interests of those contracting parties (in these cases the mothers) whose contractual status has altered in ways which they may not have predicted. They may not on their own be the proper objects of communal secular concern: but they become such by virtue of their attachment to human beings who are.

In a formal sense, this is a return to the older intrusive patterns of the past—but with one difference: whereas in the past 'society' regulated marriage in order to stabilise family life, if necessary by coercion, the task now is to manage the terms of its dissolution: and this task is to be accomplished (or at least attempted) in the context of an enhancement of individualism for all, resources permitting. This is not simply a matter of 'reconciliation' at times of stress (where by reconciliation is meant a happier goodbye) , but of so pre-emptively re-ordering the internal relations of 'the family' as to underwrite, if not actually promote, its dissolution.

As far as children are concerned, the locus classicus of this trend is the case of Gillick *vs* West Norfolk and Wisbech Area Health Authority, (Law Report October 18 1985 House of Lords). The legal point at issue was whether or not an employee of a Health Authority (a doctor or other medical personnel) could give a girl under 16 (the age of consent) contraceptive advice and treatment without her parents' knowledge and/or consent: the issue, that is, was one of parental rights.

Lord Scarman, stated that 'the present case was the beginning, not the conclusion, of a legal development in a field ('of immense consequence to our society') not yet fully explored'; he felt that the pill 'had given women a ... degree of independence greater than any law of equal opportunity could by itself effect: ... Parental rights clearly existed and did not wholly disappear until the age of majority. They related to both the person and the property of the child—custody, care and control of the person, and guardianship of the property of the child. But the common law had never treated such rights as sovereign or beyond review and control. Nor had our law ever treated the child other than as a person with capacities and rights recognised by law. Parental rights were derived from parental duty and existed only so long as they were needed for the protection of the person and property of the child.

Lord Fraser had earlier stated that: Parental rights to control the child existed not for the benefit of the parent but for the child. It was contrary to the ordinary experience of mankind, at least in Western Europe in the present century, (!!!), to say that a child remained under the complete control of his parents until he obtained the definite age of majority, and that on attaining that age he suddenly acquired independence. In practice most wise parents relaxed their control gradually as their child developed and encouraged him to become increasingly independent. Moreover the degree of parental control actually exercised over a particular child did in fact vary considerably according to his understanding and intelligence. He agreed with Lord Denning that the parents had 'a dwindling right which the courts will hesitate to enforce against the wishes of the child, and the more so the older he is. It starts with the right of control and ends with little more than advice.

Despite Lord Fraser's attempt (slightly corrected!) to present such a view as embodying the 'ordinary experience of mankind', it is clear that both he and Lord Scarman realised that they were in fact articulating a modern, twentieth century description of the relationships between parents and children. Just as women as wives are no longer seen as subsumed into the 'individuality' of the male, so children are now seen as possessing from birth an immanent or 'natural' individuality of their own which, gradually but inevitably, and as of right, lays claim to an autonomy exercisable irrespective of parental views or wishes—which are reduced to 'advice', ie. to an ignorable proffering.

The Natural Rights of Children

These 'natural rights' of children are circumscribed by no sense of 'natural obligations' of children to their parents, since only parents have obligations and duties, and obligations and duties are only what they have: their 'rights' are in essence another obligation. It is difficult to imagine a more precarious basis for parenting. In the particular case at issue, one has to imagine Mrs Gillick, exercising her 'dwindling right' to give advice to her under-age daughter, who in turn finds that advice eminently ignorable, given the more helpful 'advice' on offer from helpful medical personnel and learned law lords, who will in turn be quite popular with the under-age daughter's partner, who will no doubt be energetically exercising his rights as well, with Mrs Gillick bravely and forlornly giving advice (to who?), and giving advice, and yet more advice, there being nothing easier than giving advice to licensed ignorers who you happen to love...

The Gillick case suggests that parents encounter in their children creatures whose status inside the family is in the first resort underwritten by state functionaries (in this case medical personnel) and in the last resort by the courts. It is not as if these functionaries have to rest their case for intervening between parent and child on grounds either of greater wisdom or knowledge, although this is usually the most readily mobilised (and most demonstrably silly) justification: nor, in this particular case, did they have to prove that the parent is an actual danger to the child—the court accepted that Mrs Gillick was an exemplary mother, no matter how much she was abused in and by the gutter press.

Because the Court defined the parental contribution as 'advice', with alternative 'advice' being available from other sources, then logically *the real location of authority is now the child itself*—the child, it seems, can and should decide whether all of them should be ignored: and it should be noted that in this particular case the choice concerned is that to be made *by a minor* about sex and procreation. On such matters, parents are to see themselves as only one (admittedly an important one) of a series of advice-offerers—they will, of course, be the ones who actually live with the child, well-advised or not, advice-taking or not, successfully self-guiding or not.

It would not be surprising if parenting in this environment became a task rather sensibly avoided, if only because children educated to perceive of themselves as possessed of rights and their parents, per contra, as possessed only of obligations, might turn rather quickly into quirky little room-mates indeed. One cannot imagine, for example, sharing a flat with someone on this basis! A recent letter in *The Guardian* put the issue rather well—and note that this is from a child of the cloth (who however prefers to remain anonymous!).

The letter-writer described the miseries visited upon her because of her father's job: he was a 'smashing man', she wrote:

'but oh how often I have wished that he was doing another job. For several years I had to pop up smiling at garden parties and help out at jumble sales and children's summer clubs. And all the while I had no particular conviction of my own to carry me through.

She continued by saying that even at age thirty, married and with her own family, she 'couldn't escape the clutch of the church':

> In no other job is the family of the applicant a criteria (sic) for success. The church is employing, and paying, one person, and the rest of the family should be free to lead their own lives and have their own beliefs.[30]

The writer clearly assumes that matters in 'ordinary' (non-clerical) families are indeed as she thinks they ought to be, with members of the family, adult and juvenile, free to live lives organised on the basis of indifference to the activities of the others. (One assumes that this freedom does not extend to the person actually earning the money: if he took the same attitude there would be no family.) At the same time as these strongly centrifugal attitudes and legal decisions are effectively separating out the 'one flesh' of the family, then the Children Act seeks to reinstate, for actually separating spouses, an enforceable set of parental obligations—recognising, perhaps, that the unruly mishmash of obligations, advice and rights that 'The family' has now become is now capable of being lived with only by people who are no longer actually living together. While the amount of divorce now occurring will presumably be enough to keep all available social workers busy on such cases, there is clearly an inclination in the debates about the Children Act to set up a bench mark for 'Best Parental Practice' as a prelude to some kind of licensing system for would-be parents, of a kind already applied to adopters and foster-parents. It may well be that the 'ordinary' family is now in such disarray, and that there are now so many other parenting options, that such a licensing or surveillance system is the least worst option, a kind of Family MOT, with freedom to do what you like above the minimum standard.

The most significant way in which our society differs from all those societies analysed by anthropologists is in our lack of a coherent once-and-for-all maturation rite or ritual. No Kwakiutl or Gikuyu elder ever pretended that whole groups of young people went from being children to being adults, all in one step, simply because they all at the same time passed through some rite. Indeed, it is the very artificiality of such rituals which make them necessary and effective: they are acts of ambitious fiction, invitations to try to behave properly, not rubber stampings of or rewards for achievements already a 'matter of record.'

In the Christian culture of our part of the world, under the invasive patterns of sexual regulation described above, it was the marriage act which structured the transition from childhood to adulthood: and it was, whether as financial negotiation or as religious ceremony, an act firmly rooted in a fixed and policed set of socially-defined behaviour. Because the transition was artificial, and because life was too hard to permit of too many people being allowed to revert to childish ways (a more attractive option then and now), the uxorious community collectively supported (controlled) these once-children, now-near parents, as they began to live up to the realisation that being a parent of this child meant that being a child oneself was no longer an option: children were indeed the death of me—the old, discarded childish me, now firmly put away.

In the post-Gillick family, where children's maturation is the gradual revelation to them of the several ages at which they acquire rights rather than obligations, and the concomitant demonstration that parents have mere obligations and little authority (though an amount of power which may be used cruelly), then the moments of 'maturity' become the moments of incremental freedom from obligations, and the future becomes the promise of ever more freedom and freedoms. Children are already, within their family of origin, major influencers of family expenditure decisions; and in many middle class families have at least as much independent space and exclusive ownership of consumer durables as do their parents. The idea of 'pocket money' is as outmoded as the idea of 'pin money' to a generation of youth who are perfectly familiar long before 'maturity' with overdrafts, credit cards, holidays abroad, contraception,—and all of the other accoutrements of late twentieth century capitalism. This may well reflect the infantilisation of culture rather than an enhanced maturity of the young: but in as much as maturity is wisdom in the ways of the society of which we are part, then Mrs Gillick's children are mature indeed.

If Immanuel Todd is correct in his belief that family structure is the determinant of political culture, then one can expect that the 'Free world' will become steadily freer. It is almost impossible to imagine 'the authoritarian personality' arising out of the deconstructed relationships of contemporary family life, while the freedoms so insistently deployed therein must surely become forms of socialisation hugely indifferent to the pretensions of centralised power or demagogic politicians.

The only caveat on this must be the thought that children who experience little authority in their family life will fail to recognise authority when it presents itself in a grim, if disguised, form. Postwar discussion about 'the authoritarian personality' and 'mass society' have rather gone out of fashion and carry connotations of political manipulation which simply seem to be beyond the competence of our own politicians, even if they were inclined that way. Such manipulative competence as now exists lies with the decentralised pluralisms of the market, demanding obedience not to The One Cause but to the several pleasures. Herein, surely, lies the dilemma of contemporary capitalism: as Michael Novak puts it, the wealth of nations is most likely to increase when there is increased personal liberty[31]—which is essentially what these teenage consumers are enjoying; and while Novak then goes on to insist that 'hedonism and decadence' must be resisted with all the power that capitalism can produce (including coercion?), the problem still remains: individual freedom in economic matters will inevitably lead to individual freedom in all other aspects of life. Freedom is not divisible and a wise man can perhaps do no other than regard the sad human results of carnal excess as the moral equivalent of commercial bankruptcy—tragic for the maker of the error, but systemically useful as a warning to would-be emulators and as a sign-post to better practice in the future.

Conclusion

In all probability 'normal' marriage and family life are headed for the history books: the following five diagrams illustrate the main changes. Many centuries ago family life was lived in a rather transparent way, with supra-familial institutions such as the Church and one's kin supervising a range of decisions and activities (Figure 1) which in the modern world came to be heavily 'bounded', ie., located in the private sphere (indicated by heavy lines), within which there was in turn a clear hierarchy, with the male/husband/father being clearly dominant inside the family and responsible for its transactions with the outside (Figure 2).

It is this kind of family which is most likely to be assumed to be the norm by writers concerned with 'individualism'. Figure 3 is in part a description of how many families actually do order their internal family lives and in part an expression of how, on an optimistic assessment (which I do not share) people may be able to order their internal lives. Figure 4 seems to me to be more realistic: the broken lines, both between the outside world and between the 'members' of the family indicate the impact of the centrifugal forces—divorce, pre-marital sex, children's rights, etc.—operating today, with the state (as in Welfare State) playing an ever larger role, forcing people to be free, and with a new category (New Kin) arriving in the form of step-relations of one kind or another. Figure 5 is in part a description of how an increasing number of people do actually live now, with men no longer husbands in any sense and fathers only in the sense of casual visitors with a mere biological connection to their children and a merely nostalgic one to the mothers of those children: this is a system, or trend, of subsidised matriarchy.

In the *Relationship Revolution* published by One Plus One of the Central Middlesex Hospital, London, 1992, it is forecast that by the year 2000 living together will be the norm, that society will be matrilineal, and that the only indissoluble relationship will be that between a mother and her children. This may be a good and socially good arrangement—for some: black (predominantly West Indian/ British-born West Indian) women, as both mothers and daughters, seem to be doing remarkably well in school, college and at work, and such women tend to come from households with a long tradition of single parenting by mothers. Black men, however, are in a very different position. More generally, children from single households (most of which are female-headed) do rather worse than children from two-parent households.

US *Cosmopolitan* magazine, of January 1992 reported that 70 per cent of the mothers who lost custody of their children in divorce proceedings were 'extremely happy' while 7 per cent were 'euphoric' at being freed from the burden of motherhood; and *Elle* magazine of March 1992 seemed to have women taking a generally male view of sex (promiscuity is a good indicator of parental behaviour), when 30 per cent of their female respondents went out socially specifically looking for sex, though only 5 per cent said they would have sex on their first date. Female promiscuity (pre-marital and extra-marital) seems, by most surveys, to be approaching that of men.

It is clear that women are aware of the financial costs of motherhood; Heather Joshi, author of *Mothers Earnings* warns that going on 'the mommy track' could lose a British mother £224,000 in lost earnings. It is probably for this reason that there has been a noticeable rise in late (30+) births: by the year 2000 over 40 per cent of all births will be to women aged 30+. This may well reflect prudent parenting by women, given the Family Policy Studies Centre Fact Sheet No. 2, 1991, entitled 'An Aging Population', which stated that divorce will increase the number of isolated, ignored and financially insecure people, many of them women. By 2025 the proportion of elderly who are divorced will have quadrupled. The same Family Policy Studies Centre recently compared the life-chances of children in single parent households with those from re-constituted households (step-families), to show that children from the former do better than those from the latter—no doubt because the adults in re-constituted households are necessarily more concerned with their own relationships (which often don't work out, there being a very high re-divorce rate in such families) than with their children. As noted above, the number of children born outside formal marriage is increasing in England and Wales—over 30 per cent in 1990, compared with 13 per cent in 1981: and this in spite of a 60 per cent increase in abortion over the same years (the rate of increase of abortion for women aged 20-34 nearly doubled over the same period).

It is difficult to know whether the rapid rise in births outside marriage is the consequence of resurgent male irresponsibility, or of female inexperience in sexual licence, or a brave experiment in matriarchy, or a rite of passage for young girls denied adulthood either in the (non-existent) work-place or the unappealing male home. Whatever the reason, it is a major cause of poverty and all the attendant 'underclass' life, and a particular burden on women. Marriage for him, wrote Fay Weldon, is not the same as marriage for her: neither is parenthood in these circumstances—which are not the circumstances of affluence, but of life in a Social Security colony. The freedoms and dreams of the rich are the oppressions and nightmares of the poor—deserving or otherwise.

It is difficult to follow Lord Scarman in thinking that all this happened *because* of the Pill—unless one sees the Pill itself as a form of technology called into being by the voice and echoes of the doctrine of individualism and individual liberty. Capitalism, said Marx, 'cannot exist without constantly revolutionising the instruments of production',[32] and a co-relative factor in the transformation of procreational and erotic life in this century must surely be the huge drift from a savings-oriented capitalism, with domestic use of income determined by one (male) adult, to consumer capitalism, in which appetitive individualism and centrifugal 'relationships' are functional (indeed vital) for economic growth.

It is necessary to have recourse neither to conspiracy theories of history, nor to accord a conscious purpose to an abstraction such as 'capitalism' to note the congruency in the real world between, say, the huge pop music and disco industry and the freedom of youth (ever younger!) to have and to spend their 'own' money. A large section of the housing market relies upon both youthful independence and divorce to create demand for housing units. The sex industry—from making and filling condoms, to endless magazines and manuals, to dating agencies, to prostitution and to romantic holidays in Thailand—all create work, if not wealth: and in the employment sphere (which may or may not be the same as economic growth) serious career opportunities open up for middle class caring and policing professionals anxious to attend to the grimmer victims of the social changes of which they themselves are the more amiable and proselytising beneficiaries. Much of this employment is in the service sector, and much of it in the public sector: and much of it is female intensive, reinforcing with the power of the pay packet the clear insistence of women on increased independence.

There is of course a large amount of child labour, and certainly a larger amount of work for young people, who as purveyors and consumers of trend and fashion are a dominant presence in the market place. In addition, the rapid expansion of further education has created widespread 'leaving home' facilities (called Universities) ie. a way of leaving home which minimises, by appealing to mutual self-interest, the inter-generational frictions experienced by the Crusoes. Here again, women are major beneficiaries, the most radical alteration in University life in particular being the arrival of a student body of which over half are female. (They are all, of course, children.)

Whatever the causes, there has been a huge increase in me-too individualism and the concomitant liberties: just as the nuclear family extracted itself out of the kinship network in order to lay claim to the pleasures, responsibilities and privileges of privacy and liberty, so now have the members of that nuclear family extracted themselves out of those restricted relationships with each other within it in order to lay claim to the responsibilities and privileges of individual autonomy and liberty. As Abraham Lincoln said of the society of which he was President: the issue is whether a society so founded (on equality and liberty) can long endure. The issue is not simply whether our society can live with a form of family life which is very different from what we had before—such as, for analogy, changing from a selective education system to a non-selective system. The issue is whether our society can live with no system at all. That is to say, can we, within the overwhelming ethos of **Privacy and Appetitive Individualism**, accept an endless variety of sexual and procreative relationships which lack both internal stability and a clear articulation within society in general. In the past, as our progenitors coped with (say) the huge social transformations of the industrial and urban revolutions, the essential family unit (in ideal at least) retained a unity and indeed gave to the socially mobile classes the vital grounding in ability to deal with change and novelty, with emigration and social advancement, with unpredictable exigencies and anticipated troubles. Even in its frictions—crucially, the oedipal-like centrifugal frictions between fathers and sons—the family operated as a system integrated with and to some extent controlling and remaking the world of which it was part. It could well be that the world now requires less of a concentrated imperialist effort: and that the casual transactions of 'relationships' are what the age—The Age of Aquarius—demands. It is certainly what its getting.

Michael Novak notes that:

> classic theoreticians of the 'new order of the world' did not write at length, profoundly or with unmitigated admiration of the family ..(because) the great intellectual breakthroughs of the modern era occurred, rather, around the polar concepts of the *individual* and the *state*.. The discoverers of 'the natural system of liberty' stressed the distinctive, aspiring *individual* and the self-limiting *state* that would liberate his energies. For generations, political theory, economic theory and moral theory—preoccupied with the individual and the state—have systematically neglected the social vitality of the family.[33]

It would, of course, be obviously quite wrong to argue that the 'classic theoreticians' referred to by Novak (he mentions John Locke, Adam Smith, and John Stuart Mill) took no interest in family matters or in the male/female issue, but one has also to agree with Novak that their writings must be seen more in terms of what they wrote *against* than in terms of what they wrote *about*. We still lack an effective over-all theoretical and moral framework for the functioning of the family in the modern world.

The story of marriage in our contemporary world is one of the abstraction of the individual from these systems of social support and control. Marriage is now the great romantic act: everything ventured on one great gesture of individualism, with no attention at all being paid to the wider kin, very little (none if that is the way it has to be) to close kin; and not very much to anything other than the most formal of religious or societal obligations. The logic of this drive to individualise the marriage decision is of course the drive to individualise the marital relationship itself, with both spousal and parental obligations being increasingly regarded as matters of taste and fashion rather than of permanent social commitment.

With such a belief, derision can be poured on, say, the earlier view (taken as common sense by our predecessors) that promiscuity before marriage will result in unfaithfulness during marriage. On the contrary, the authenticity of the earlier promiscuousness, say the modernists, will simply become the authenticity of faithfulness—it is the experience by **The Self** of its authenticity which will see at least *that* Self through *this* problem, for the time being...

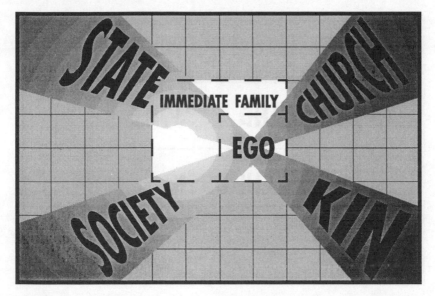

Figure 1

Figure 2

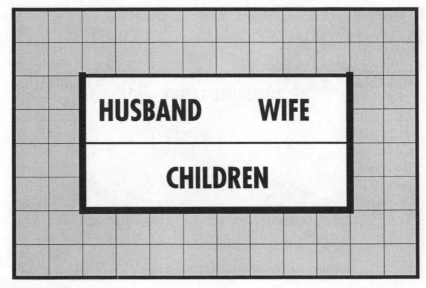

Figure 3

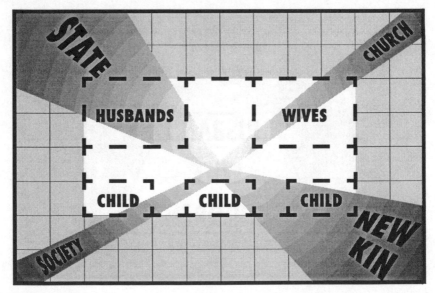

Figure 4

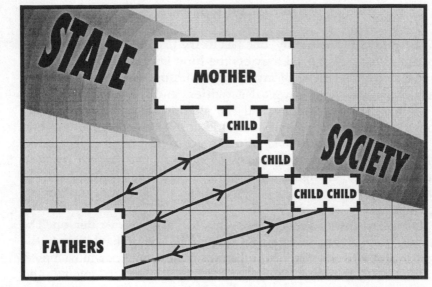

Figure 5

Bibliographical Note

In the study of 'The Family' one has to try to carry in one's mind the fixities of biology, if fixed they be: the long imprint of pre-history or archaeology, the lessons of mythology, anthropology and of complex religious rituals and liturgical activities: and the great social and economic changes which made the modern world and which are now conjuring up, in an exciting and amazing way, a post-modern era. The 'modern' family is a recent construct, rooted in all of the above, for better or for worse, but like so much of the modern (or post modern) world, changing much more quickly than it ever seems to have done in the past. The discontinuities are now greater than the continuities.

In the last fifteen years more seems to have been written on 'The Family' than on any other single subject. This is probably due to the power and effectiveness of the Feminist movement, or movements, as well as to the very obvious and rapid increase in divorce (and separation) and in single parenthood due to both divorce and to births outside of wedlock. In addition there are the associated phenomena of well-documented widespread sexual activity among the very young, a radical transformation in the whole 'discourse' about sex, in both pornography, weekly magazines and the other mass media, and an anxious concern about the latest form of venereal disease, AIDS. It should be noted that in the midst of all these disturbing changes, marriage, parenting and family life retain their value for both the British and other European people: see both *British Social Attitudes*, Gower publications, edited annually by Roger Jowell and *Contrasting Values in Western Europe* (part of the European Values Study Group), edited by Stephen Harding et al., Macmillan 1986. The writings of Michael Argyle (for example *The Psychology of Happiness*, Routledge, 1987) demonstrate very conclusively how the set of relationships known as 'family' are central to our well-being and social functioning.

In many ways—and not only sexually—contemporary family life seems to be more securely grounded in mutual benefit and satisfaction than it was, say forty or fifty years ago: properly representative surveys of such matters are not much older than that, but from both Steven Humphries's *A Secret World of Sex— Forbidden Fruit, The British Experience 1900-1950*, (Sidgwick and Jackson, 1988) and Geoffrey

Gorer's *Sex and Marriage in England Today* (Nelson, 1971) it would be easy to derive a picture of an anxious and repressed and narrowly male-centred family life. Such surveys, of course, were limited both in what could be asked and in what people would answer: and it may well be that an historian of Peter Gay's competence may have given a gentler picture of family life forty or fifty years ago: see Peter Gay, *Education of the Senses: The Bourgeois Experience, Victoria to Freud,* (OUP, 1984), in particular the bibliographical essay at the end of the book. A neo-marxist historian of the same era is Jeffrey Weeks' *Sex Politics and Society: The Regulation of Sexuality since 1800,* (Longmans, 1981). *Prosperity and Parenthood,* by John Banks, (Routledge, 1954) deals with middle class family planning activities—and much else.

McGregor's *Divorce in England* (Heinemann, 1957) is a bit dated but provides a wealth of data. The excellent series produced over the years by what is now The Family Policy Studies Centre provide enough figures for anyone who would to read: see in particular *Family Change and Future Policy,* by Kathleen Kiernan and Malcolm Wicks (Family Policy Studies Centre, 1991).

The historical arguments go back well beyond the 'Bourgeois Experience', and are still best summarised in Michael Anderson's *A History of the Western Family 1500 to 1914* (Penguin, 1980). John Gillis deals specifically with marriage (*For Better or For Worse, British Marriages, 1600 to the Present,* OUP, 1985). Edward Shorter's *The Making of the Modern Family* (Fontana/Collins, 1975) is one of the better general histories. Lawrence Stone, *Road to Divorce* (OUP, 1990) is a worthy successor to McGregor. Alan Macfarlane's *The Origin of English Individualism* (Blackwells, 1978) makes one realise that generalisations about kin and individual must cover rather lengthy time-scales if they are to be persuasive; indeed, writers on family and sexual matters have to be as much anthropologist as historian, and as much archaeologist as theologian if the full transformation of such matters is to be understood. From that point of view, the great Marxist classic, *The Origin of the Family, Private Property and The State* (Penguin, 1989) is still an inspiring model, even though the zeal of the polemicist runs well ahead of reality.

The best single book on parents and children is a book by that name—*Parents and Children, the Ethics of the Family,* by Jeffrey Blustein (OUP, 1982): while John Eekelaar's *Family Law and Social Policy* (and other writings by the same author) (Weidenfeld and Nicolson, 1978) deals with the grounds and nature of public intervention at times of family breakdown.

Sexual ethics were for many hundreds of years the preserve of the Church: and Tentler's *Sin and Confession on the Eve of the Reformation* (Princeton U.P., 1977); Payer's *Sex and the Penitentials, the Development of a Sexual Code 550-1150* (University of Toronto Press, 1984) outline the historical functioning of a systematic ethic of social control, the logic of which can be understood by reference to John T. Noonan's *Contraception—A History of its Treatment by Catholic Theologians and Canonists* (Cambridge, Mass., 1965), and by Joseph Kern, *The Theology of Marriage: the Historical Development of Christian Attitudes towards Sex and Sanctity in Marriage* (Sheed and Ward, 1964). Noonan's title is misleading—the book is a general overview of Catholic teaching. A modern defence of Catholic teaching—a teaching which, it must be stressed, is systematic in nature and therefore not susceptible to being changed in increments—is *Catholic Sexual Ethics*, by Lawler et. al (OSV, Indiana, 1985). John Paul the Second's *Familiaris Consortio: the Christian Family in the Modern World* (Catholic Truth Society, 1981) restates the historic message. Anglican perspectives are *Marriage Divorce and the Church* (SPCK, 1971); and the development of the liturgy is to be found in Lowther Clarke, *Liturgy and Worship* (SPCK, 1932). W.E. Tate's *The Parish Chest* and W.G. Hoskins *The Midland Peasant* (MacMillan, 1957), together with books such as Quaife's *Wanton Wenches and Wayward Wives* (Croom Helm, 1979) give a good picture of what sexual life was like 'in those days', and should perhaps be read in conjunction with Peter Laslett's *The World We Have Lost* (3rd edition, Methuen, 1983) and Keith Thomas's *Religion and the Decline of Magic* (Penguin, 1988). The great Dictionaries and Encyclopedias of religion and ethics contain a large amount of wisdom, well packaged.

Freud seems to me to be absolutely essential reading; and among the best 'users' of Freud are Peter Gay and Talcott Parsons. The latter's *Family Socialisation and Interaction Process* is still the best account of the family as a small group—an obvious point, but most often taken after it has been made. Kate Millett's *Sexual Politics* (Virago, 1985), is a witty and potent Freudian debunker of much male literature—D.H. Lawrence gets put in his place. Fay Weldon's books are disturbingly perceptive; see, for example, *Praxis* (Hodder and Stoughton, 1978).

Jack Goody's *The Development of the Family and Marriage in Europe* (OUP, 1983) brings a blend of history and anthropology to bear on the relations between the Church and family matters. Alan Macfarlane's *The Origins of English Individualism*, already referred to, makes one aware of the slow-moving nature of change in family affairs. The Marriage Act of 1753 was a very late 'end' to the medieval period when it introduced some degree of secular regulation of marriage, and before that there is probably more variation than uniformity in the British national system. Simon Schama's *The Embarrassment of Riches* (Fontana, 1988) is a superb account of the rise of the bourgeoisie, while Pierre Darmon's very amusing *Trial by Impotence* (The Hogarth Press, 1985) is in some measure at least a description of the world the bourgeoisie was intent on moving away from!

Bryan Turner (Blackwell, 1984) and Peter Brown (Faber, 1989) have both written a book with the same title—*The Body and Society*—and to some extent share the same carnal concern, although from rather different points of view; Turner is more interested in a general anthropology of the body, while Brown's book is about early Christian experiences of celibacy and chastity. This latter theme is also covered by Ranke-Heinemann in *Eunuchs for Heaven* (Andre Deutsch, 1990). The Venerable Bede's *History of the English Church and People* describes the nature of Christian missionary activity, which probably varies little from those days to these. Readers interested in Biblical sources will find various references in Genesis, 1:26-27, 2, all, 3, all; Matthew, 5:27-32, 10:21-37, 19:3-19 and 29; Mark, 10:1-12, 29-31, 12:19-26; 1 Corinthians, 5,6,7, all; Ephesians, 5, all, 6:1-7; Colossians, 3:18-23; Titus, 2, all. *Familiaris Consortio*, from the Catholic Truth Society, deals with the 'Christian Family in the Modern World'. This should be read in conjunction with *Centesimus Annus* (1991) which provides a Catholic appreciation of the contemporary world. The most evocative representation of this world is still—if only because of its title—David Riesman's *The Lonely Crowd* (Yale University Press, 1950).

Notes

1 The Venerable Bede, *History of the English Church and People*, Book 1, Ch. 27, Penguin edition, 1968, p. 77.

2 Kramer, Heinrich and Sprenger, James, *Malleus Maleficarum*, first published in 1496 and re-issued in 1986 by Arrow Books.

3 Tentler, T., *Sin and Confession on the Eve of the Reformation*, Princetown University Press, 1977, p. 206.

4 *Malleus Maleficarum, op. cit.*, p. 140.

5 The Anglican *Book of Common Prayer*, 1662 version.

6 Ozment, S., *When Fathers Ruled*, Harvard University Press, 1983, p. 6.

7 Marx and Engels, *The Communist Manifesto*, Penguin edition, 1985, p. 82.

8 Novak, M., *The Spirit of Democratic Capitalism*, 1991, p. 158.

9 *Ibid.*

10 *An Outline for Boys and Girls and their Parents*, (ed) Mitchison, Naomi, Gollancz, 1932, p. 165.

11 Bunyan, John,*The Pilgrim's Progress*, London: Sunday School Union, undated, p. 19.

12 Defoe, Daniel, *Robinson Crusoe*, Macmillan, 1905.

13 Swift, Jonathan, *Gulliver's Travels—Part 4*, A voyage to the Country of the Houyhnhnms, The World's Classics, 1902, p. 277.

14 Hayek, F.A., *Individualism and Economic Order*, RKP., 1949, p. 13.

15 Smith, Adam, *The Wealth of Nations*, vol. 2, Bk.5, (ed) Edwin Cannan, Methuen, 1950, p. 266.

16 Rathbone, Eleanor, *The Disinherited Family*, Ed. Arnold, 1924.

17 Novak, M., *The Spirit of Democratic Capitalism*, London: Institute of Economic Affairs, 1991, pp. 160-166.

18 Todd, Immanuel, *The Explanation of Ideology—Family Structures and Social System*, Blackwell, 1985, p. 6.

19 Tillich, Paul, *The Courage To Be*, Collins, 1962.

20 Thomas a Kempis, *The Imitation of Christ*, Penguin, 1952.

21 Talcott Parsons, *Family Socialisation and Interaction Process*, RKP., 1956.

22 Gay, Peter, *The Bourgeois Experience—Victoria to Freud: vol.1, Education of the Senses*, OUP., 1984.

23 Light, Allison, *Forever England: Femininity, Literature and Conservatism Between the Wars*, Routledge, 1992.

24 Talcott Parsons, *op. cit.*, chapter one.

25 Gorer, Geoffrey, *Sex and Marriage in England Today*, Nelson, 1971.

26 Humphries, Steve, *A Secret World of Sex—Forbidden Fruit: the British Experience 1900-1950*, Sidgwick and Jackson, 1988.

27 Young, Michael and Willmott, Peter, *The Symmetrical Family*, p. 270.

28 Hayek, F.A., *The Constitution of Liberty*, RKP, 1976, p. 451.

29 *The Newcastle Journal*, 6 March 1992.

30 Letter, *The Guardian* newspaper, 14 May 1992.

31 Novak, M., *op. cit.*, pp. 102-3.

32 *The Communist Manifesto, op. cit.*, p. 83.

33 Novak, M., *op. cit.*, pp. 159-60.

The Moral Foundations of Market Institutions

John Gray   **£7.95**   **142pp**

"This powerful tract ... is persuasive"   **Andrew Adonis, Financial Times**

"one of the most intelligent and sophisticated contributions to conservative philosophy"   **Roger Scruton, The Times**

In *The Moral Foundations of Market Institutions*, John Gray, the distinguished Oxford philosopher, examines the moral legitimacy of the market economy. His contribution is particularly timely as leaders of the former East European communist states and the new republics of the erstwhile Soviet Union turn to the West for understanding of the elements which make possible a free society.

The book also includes thee critical commentaries by Professor Patrick Minford, Chandran Kukathas and Professor Raymond Plant.

The Spirit of Democratic Capitalism

Michael Novak   **£7.95**   **463pp**

"Novak...has done us a service in illuminating where the fault lines between right and left now lie."   **Will Hutton, The Guardian**

"Mr Major...might seek inspiration from The Spirit of Democratic Capitalism by Michael Novak"   **Joe Rogaly, Financial Times**

The Spirit of Democratic Capitalism has become a classic work in the study of free societies. The book's powerful advocacy of democratic capitalism led it to be frequently reprinted in Latin America and to its underground (samizdat) publication by Solidarity in Poland, in which form it was read by the present Pope. The language of his most recent encyclical, Centesimus Annus suggests that Pope John Paul II has absorbed much of Novak's thought and style.

It is Novak's challenging contention that, contrary to its many critics, capitalism is not only pragmatically superior but morally more sound than any other alternative that the world has to offer. Michael Novak reconciles the moral, theological and spiritual underpinnings of capitalism heretofore unarticulated and defies socialism to claim the moral high ground.